MICROGREENS

GORDON L. ATWELL

An Essential Guide to Grow Nutrient-Dense Organic Microgreens for Your Health or Profit

Gordon L. Atwell

financial, medical or professional advice. The content within this book has been derived from various sources. Please consult a licensed professional before attempting any techniques outlined in this book.

By reading this document, the reader agrees that under no circumstances is the author responsible for any losses, direct or indirect, that are incurred as a result of the use of the information contained within this document, including, but not limited to, errors, omissions, or inaccuracies.

TABLE OF CONTENTS

INTRODUCTION

D o you want to get healthy, strong, and vital, with only a handful of plants daily? Perhaps you're familiar with microgreens, and you want to grow them. If you're unfamiliar with these popular plants but want to find out more, this book will give you the right answers! If you know a good deal about microgreens and want to learn to grow them like a pro, this book will even show you how to turn your kitchen hobby into a six-figure business! This book aims to provide you with all essential information needed for understanding microgreens, their origin and history, benefits, and best use. Once you're finished with this book, you'll be equipped with thorough knowledge to use and cultivate these gentle herbs to your greatest benefit.

This book will present you with explanations, tips, and strategies for growing and consuming microgreens, whether for personal use or commercially. This book will help you if you're looking to improve your diet or only looking to find out more about the newly-discovered superfood. If you want to grow your own garden, this book will give you thorough instructions for cultivation of microgreens, from choosing the variety and seeds, to planting, harvesting, and storing. If you're looking to start a business with microgreens, this book will give you the exact advice on what you need to do to commercialize the small plant production.

Moreover, you will find out how microgreens can improve your health, all based on study of scientific research. In this book, we reviewed only reliable, science-based information and facts, to give you only the best instructions and strategies. This book resulted from a detailed review of best practices, recommendations, and research projects dedicated to studying microgreens. As a result of their growing popularity, researchers worldwide are trying to figure out whether the hype surrounding the plants is justified, or they're simply a trend that will pass with the "next big thing."

First, you'll learn what exactly microgreens are. To be able to make your own judgment about microgreens, you'll first learn their definition, after which you'll find out about their history, development, and rise in popularity. The first chapter of this book will tell you whether the hype around microgreens revolves around fiction, or if the cultivation of the varieties has been around for a long time, and they're just now receiving due attention. With this knowledge, you'll be better able to understand the culture and history behind microgreens and know how to distinguish genuine, accurate information from false advertising that aims to dig into your wallet. Once you start to understand the history behind microgreens, you'll proceed to learn about their nutritional benefits.

Once you start to learn about the health benefits of using microgreens, which you'll find in the second chapter of this book, it will become clearer why microgreens are esteemed as they are. You'll learn what science discovered about the nutritional value of these herbs, and what the greatest health benefits are from using them. Here, you'll learn how you can improve your health using targeted microgreens, and why they're so powerful when it comes to supporting not only a healthy diet but also recovery from many illnesses. With this knowledge, you'll be better able to understand how to use these plants to improve your well-being and target specific health areas that need extra support.

Once you've learned how exactly you can benefit from microgreens, you'll learn how to choose the best plants and top-quality seeds. As you'll learn, seeds have enormous value for a future crop. Any farmer will tell you that the quality of the crop depends on the quality of the seed. In the third chapter of this book, you'll learn not only why seeds matter in cultivation of microgreens but also how to find and choose top-quality seeds. Once you learn that, I'll show you how to take good care of your seeds to preserve their shelf life and protect them from decay. With this know-ledge, you'll be able to cultivate microgreens with certainty and confidence that you're giving them the best chance to grow.

After this, you'll learn how to plant and culti-vate microgreens step-by-step. In this book, you will find the exact instructions needed for easy-breezy microgreen cultivation. You'll find out what exact tools and supplies are needed, and you'll also learn how to plant, maintain, harvest, and store the crops properly. With this in mind, you will be completely equipped to start growing microgreens right now!

In the fourth chapter of this book, you will learn what exact tools and supplies you need to grow healthy microgreens. In this book, you will also learn more about how to get the right containers, watering systems, fertilizers, and lighting to grow healthy and nutritious microplants. After this, you will learn about the very process of growing microgreens.

In this chapter, you will also learn the right steps for growing microgreens, from obtaining seeds to planting them in the trays and the process of har-vesting. This will help you get ready to do your own creative work while choosing the species that you will love and enjoy. Finally, you will learn how to provide your plants with the best conditions to thrive in terms of lighting, supplementation, temperature, hygiene, and more. With this knowledge, you will prevent withering and contamination of your plants and produce an optimum number of healthy crops from the seeds you purchase.

In the fifth chapter of this book, you will learn how to properly eat and use microgreens. To experience the true health benefits from microgreens, you have to know how to store and use them properly. First things first, we will tell you how to make microgreens a steady part of your daily diet. We will show you how to incorporate them into common meals to enrich their flavor and nutritional value. You will also learn how to cook microgreens properly to preserve their nutrients and intensify the taste that they will release into your meals.

Last but not least, you will find out how to turn your microgreen hobby into a business. If you stay persistent in following the guidelines from this book, you will easily be able to grow your own healthy crops. Once you're certain of your knowledge, you will be able to grow greater amounts and profit from your work. The final chapter of this book will guide you through establishing and maintaining a microgreen business. First, we will explain how and why microgreens are profitable and what you can do to enhance the profits from starting your own business. We will first explain what the advantages are of growing microgreens for sale and how you can start doing it using the tools and supplies you already have in your home.

Next, we will give you exact calculations of possible profits and startup costs for a microgreen business. With this knowledge, you will be able to determine whether you'll be satisfied with small production and keeping your cultivation as a hobby, or you want to aim for bigger goals and conquer the market. Next, we will show you how to properly sell microgreens. As with any other business, selling microgreens will require adjusting to the rules of the market. We will show you how to evaluate your competition and learn from them to improve the quality of your own crops. Next, we'll show you how to maintain a good relationship with your customers so that your brand becomes visible and grows in popularity and profitability. With this knowledge, you will be fully equipped to not only grow and eat microgreens for optimal health benefits but to also grow your own income. Thank you for taking the time to read this book! We hope you will enjoy it and find it invaluable.

CHAPTER 1: WHAT ARE MICROGREENS, AND WHY GROW THEM?

Welcome to the first chapter of your manual for growing and using microgreens! If you've picked up this book, you are probably at least a little bit aware of what microgreens are and how to use them.

But, do you know everything you need to cultivate them on your own? Probably not. Plant cultivation requires attention and knowledge of individual species, growth calendar, planting, and proper conditions needed for successful growth of rich-tasting, nutrient-boosting plants. Perhaps you are only interested in finding out how to successfully plant pots of micro basil, onion, or celery? Or, you want to transform your diet, and you're looking for ways to add more nutrition to your daily meals?

It could be that you see a business opportunity in growing microgreens and want to find out how to produce and sell them on a large scale. Whatever your motivation is, this book will provide the answers.

First things first, you'll need to learn the very basics to be able to understand microgreens. In this chapter, you'll first find out what microgreens are and what distinguishes them from the regular vegetables and spices you find on grocery store shelves.

With that understanding, it will become clearer what makes these small plants so special and why they are worth the effort. You'll also learn about some complications that come with large-scale produce and a couple of vulnerabilities that make these plants attention worthy.

More than that, you will learn the history behind microgreens. In this chapter, you will also learn where microgreens came from and how they came to be as popular as they are today. With this knowledge, you'll better understand how to interpret the information about their value and be able to distinguish real benefits from targeted advertising.

Here, you will learn why, despite being so simple to grow, these plants become very expensive to obtain unless you grow them on your own. With this knowledge, you'll be able to better understand the benefits they can offer but also a couple of drawbacks to industrial production. Without further ado, we'll begin our manual with some basic information about microgreens.

WHAT ARE MICROGREENS?

Microgreens are small, young greens that are grown and used to enrich the flavor of numerous dishes.

These plants are grown until they reach the first hue leaf stage and are then harvested and sold (Kyriacou et al., 2016). They belong to a species of plants that are typically harvested and consumed either in baby stages or as sprouts.

Microgreens are a third category of herbs and contain seed leaves, or cotyledons, along with stems. Most often, they're used for salads, smoothies, and as additions to numerous other dishes to enrich the flavor and boost the nutritional value of an otherwise regular dish.

While there's no legal definition for either microgreens or baby greens, you'll typically recognize them as being up to two inches tall depending on the species. Much like sprouts (e.g., pumpkin and almond), where you'll consume either the shoot, root, or seeds, microgreens share the same vulnerability to microbe contamination. In addition, they're fragile and sensitive but valuable for their vibrant color, strong flavors, and distinct textures.

Compared with microgreens, sprouts are only partially germinated. This means that they only contain the seed, root, and the stem, while a microgreen doesn't contain the root.

Compared to sprouts, microgreens are more intense in flavor, with wider selections of colors, textures, and shapes. Simply put, microgreens are a slightly more grown version of a sprout.

To grow microgreens, you'll use materials called substrates that resemble soil, and you'll need to provide them with enough sunlight to increase their nutritional value and support healthy growth.

Sun and water are the two most important elements that help the plants process the nutrients absorbed from soil to not only grow but also synthesize the substances we find to be so precious and beneficial to the diet. In addition, to grow microgreens, you will use less seed density, meaning that only a couple of seeds will be enough for growth.

Microgreens usually grow anywhere from two to six weeks, with expanded leaves signifying that the time to harvest has come. If you're purchasing microgreens, you'll often find them sold in pots while not yet fully developed.

This is to avoid oversaturation of the plant, giving you the opportunity to cut it later as you need. However, keep in mind that you should only purchase microgreens for quick use, as they lose color and flavor with maturation.

While microgreens are less labor intensive than sprouts, they come with somewhat bigger risks from pathogens and safety concerns.

This increases the probability of safety risks due to factors like the lack of knowledge of good practices, overly dense seeds, insufficient light and air, and ignoring recommended safety procedures.

There is also a probability of accidentally growing toxic plants, as some of the species—like nightshade plants that include potatoes, tomatoes, and eggplants—can become toxic.

There's a lot of variety when it comes to the taste of microgreens. While a common assumption is that they lack flavor, the truth is that they can be very spicy and sweet to the palate. They're commonly considered to be a "superfood" due to the high amount of nutrients they contain in small amounts.

They are also popular due to simplicity and ease of growth, the reasons which make them desirable for personal cultivating. You'll find species like arugula, cabbage, kale, beet, kohlrabi, amaranth, swiss chard, radish, and mustard equally as home grown plants and as a seasoning in expensive dishes in prominent restaurants that feature extravagant cuisines.

Currently, nearly 100 species are known to be grown as microgreens, including common plants like celery, buckwheat, sweet pea, spinach, lemongrass, fennel, broccoli, onions, chives, and basil, and also plants like carrots, arugula, and cress.

While growing microgreens in the comfort of your home isn't at all demanding and difficult, marketing is quite a different story. If you want to sell greens, you have to be aware of all the intricacies of not only mass production but also complex production strategies that produce the maximum amount of quality produce to sell.

Since harvesting times depend on the species, their growth calendar doesn't care much for demands of the market. While minding successful production, you'd also have to be considerate of the revenue flow that will supply the funds to settle financial duties and taxes.

With this in mind, the best advice is to focus production on the crops with similar harvesting times so that you can harvest and sell them all at once. In addition, you have the choice of planting different seeds and mixing them up after harvest.

As you can see, there are numerous options and considerations to think about when contemplating growing microgreens.

However, their nutritional value and the opportunity to enrich your life and diet with the replenishing substances they're known to possess make them worthy of studying and growing. In the next section, you'll find out more about the history of microgreen cultivation.

HISTORY OF CULTIVATION

Nowadays, microgreens are known for their nutritional value and satiating flavors that can turn a plain dish into a delicacy. But, what's the history behind microgreens?

While microgreens turned popular in mainstream culture only a couple of decades ago, rising from home-grown specimens to the secret ingredient of upscale culinary establishments, their quality and variety of uses range further back in history.

While the use of sprouts and baby plants ranges back to ancient societies, the cultivation of microgreens is fairly new. Their popularity first arose with the insight into the potential of adding flavor to otherwise plain dishes, while subsequent studies proved their nutritional benefits.

The production of microgreens across the US began in the 1990s, spreading from San Francisco and other parts of California. As with most innovations, the cultivation began in small yards, only to spread and become an industry to supply food chains and restaurants.

Here, the most popular crops included basil, arugula, kale, beets, cilantro, and a popular Rainbow Mix. They're now being grown across not only the US but also the rest of the world.

Aside from natural plants grown in homes and gardens, microgreens are found in numerous other forms, like cellulose pulp, which has been present in Europe since 2002. However, sales of living microgreens are just becoming popular, as more and more people are aware of their benefits and ease of cultivation.

However, living microgreens are rarely found in stores because of higher costs and smaller yields that impact production and packaging. In addition, large-scale production and shipping tend to negatively impact the quality of produce, due to the difficulty of keeping the plants hydrated and nourished enough to preserve the flavor and nutrients.

With added costs that come from industrial production and packaging, commercial use of fresh microgreens on a large scale remains a challenge. However, they can come at a somewhat luxurious price when grown organically in greenhouses.

The use of fresh microgreens is challenging for restaurant owners as well, since they quickly decay after being harvested and refrigerated. For this reason, systems and strategies for large-scale commercial growth are still being developed. Meanwhile, home cultivation remains a primary source of healthy flavor for individuals interested in these plants.

But, what makes these small plants so popular? What are the reasons for increased interest in their cultivation and possible health benefits? In the next section, you'll find out more about what lies behind the popularity of microgreens and what makes them a so-called "superfood."

WHY MICROGREENS BECAME POPULAR

Nowadays, the nutritional benefits of microgreens are well known, and their cultivation makes an attractive hobby for those looking to refresh their kitchens with fresh-smelling herbs grown by their own hands.

Aside from that, the small plants are getting attention and are heavily featured in culinary shows, popular cookbooks, nutritionists' recommendations, and diet plans for those looking to lose weight and get rid of fat and cholesterol. Simply put, they're all present, from farmers' markets, to TV.

This had led to an increased interest in their growth and cultivation, driving people to further learn about the art of microgreen growing. However, there are more factors contributing to their popularity than simply mainstream trending.

A rich taste is one of the biggest reasons why

microgreens became popular in the first place. Naturally, the flavor of young plants is stronger than that of the adult's, and their quick growth only contributed to the hype. Aside from that, the richness in flavor comes in the compact form of a little stem that offers vibrant tastes that range from sweetness to spiciness and are dispropor-tionate to their size.

Nutritional value is a benefit beyond question when it comes to growing microgreens. In fact, plants that are harvested in the microgreen stage tend to contain 40% more nutrients than adult plants. However, this comes at a price.

Arguably, greater quantities need to be planted and harvested with small plants to achieve the same amounts and volume that one would have with adult plants. This small obstacle can be eas-ily surpassed with their quick growth.

Within only a couple of weeks, the tiny plants are ready for use and are also suitable to grow on small spaces, like kitchen countertops. They don't require typical gardening equipment and skills, such as taking care of the soil, hydration, and fertilizing. Instead, simply planting them into a substrate of your choice and watering regularly will suffice to enjoy lush, healthy produce.

Aesthetic appeal is among the reasons why many homeowners love microgreens. They spread ador-able fragrance and can serve as decoration in kitchens and dining rooms.

Many look at them as an art, carefully planning to build stations and choose decorative pots for their small plants, to add not only scent and flavor but also a touch of freshness into the ambience of their living space.

Whether you find microgreens appealing as decor, or you simply want to add more flavor to your food without continuously having to buy spices, microgreens will provide more than a treat for the eye and the palate. Compared to fully-grown vegetables, they are richer in many vitamins, like C, E, and A.

They can be a quick and easy way to improve your diet, with larger concentrations of vitamins and minerals in small doses. On the other hand, they are a low-calorie food that allow you to enjoy taste without fearing gaining weight. In fact, they average only 29 calories per 100 grams. However, one thing to consider is that you'll have to purchase or grow greater amounts of microgreens to reap the health benefits.

With an average of 75 grams being recommended for daily use, just sprinkling the greens over your salad isn't enough to make a noticeable dietary impact. In this case, it remains up to you to decide whether the investment is worthwhile.

In this chapter, you learned what microgreens are and what makes them so popular. You learned that there's nothing specific about these small plants except the fact that they are harvested at the microstage of growth, where they contain the highest percentage of nutrients and the most intense flavor.

However, you also learned that the consistent use of these plants can become a bit of a luxury, considering the amounts that need to be consumed for health benefits.

You also learned that, despite mainstream hype created around so-called superfoods, there are many challenges to their production and harvesting.

First things first, microgreens include many species, of which each has their own time of the year to grow and be harvested. From the beginning, this shows that cultivating microgreens will require thoughtful planning. With this in mind, proceed reading this book while staying aware that the best choice is to choose the species of interest and plan their production in accordance with that.

In this chapter, you also learned that the majority of the hype surrounding microgreens comes from nutritional benefits one can enjoy with a little bit of time and effort.

But, what are these benefits? Are microgreens truly as healthy as one might assume, or does the attention surrounding them come from advertising and exaggerated claims? We will review these aspects in the following chapter, where you'll learn more about the potential health benefits of microgreens.

In the next chapter, you'll learn what makes microgreens so healthy, about their nutritional value, and what health benefits you can expect from regular use. With this knowledge, you'll be able to make an educated decision about the exact species you want to grow and the amounts you want to produce.

CHAPTER 2: NUTRITIONAL AND HEALTH BENEFITS OF MICROGREENS

I n the previous chapter, you learned what microgreens are and what makes them so popular. You learned that their intense flavor and convenience of growth has made them highly desirable both for personal and commercial cultivation during the past couple of decades.

However, the nutritional value of these gentle plants remains one of the biggest reasons why people are so eager to grow and use them. The nutritional value of microgreens has been intensely studied recently, with research examining many different varieties and individual species to measure their nutritional value and conditions for optimal growth.

I will now present you with scientifically proven

information about the health and nutritional benefits of microgreens.

After all, you are probably interested in microgreens due to their nutritional potency. Nowadays, both agriculture and medical experts are looking into the potential of microgreens to contribute to a sustainable, simple, and easy, yet optimally healthy diet.

For this reason, numerous industries, from agriculture to medicine, and even economists, have been studying the potentials of microgreens and their implications for modern eating habits, human health, and the food industry.

The research I came across mainly revolved around the potential and optimal use of these low-maintenance plants for personal and commercial purposes, and measuring their quality when produced on small farms, served at restaurants, and sold on store shelves.

In this chapter, we will explain the proven health benefits of using microgreens. We will first look into studies that examined the nutritional compounds found in different microgreens and compare them to regular fruits and vegetables.

With this knowledge, you will know exactly why microgreens are worth the effort. You will find out more about their potential to enrich your diet with nutrients that are otherwise hard to preserve in regular vegetables that can't be eaten raw.

As they don't require cooking, nutrients are pre-served that would otherwise decay while baking or boiling, which would otherwise be required in order to prepare regular vegetables.

The information given in this chapter will show you the exact nutrients you can directly ingest from only small amounts of microgreens.

Further, we'll present you with the nutritional richness of the most popular microgreen species, aiming to present you with those that have proven to contain the most abundant number of nutrients, yet remain the most practical to grow and cultivate at home.

With this knowledge, you will be equipped to obtain the right supplies and purchase the right seeds of these plants and start growing them right now. As you will learn, growing these nutritional bombs is super easy, even when done on your kitchen counter. With the information and instructions given in this chapter, you will be able to start growing your own favorite microgreens right now.

In addition, you will find out how exactly your health benefits from a daily dose of microgreens. From simply boosting your immune system to avoiding seasonal flu, to getting more fiber to improve your digestion and speed up weight loss, and even improving your blood pressure and cardiovascular health, you will learn which exact plants you can use to to alleviate issues that might be bothering you.

Whether you decide to cultivate at home or purchase microgreens from your local farmer's market or grocery store, you will know the exact species to choose for your own health and nutritional needs.

WHY ARE
MICROGREENS
SO HEALTHY?

When it comes to the nutritional value of microgreens, researchers measured a couple of nutrients that are thought to be vital for human health. Here are some of the most potent micro- and macronutrients found to be abundant in microgreens (Xiao et al., 2012; Choe & Wan, 2018).

VITAMIN K

One of the nutrients known to benefit blood coagulation is phylloquinone or vitamin K1. This nutrient is most often found in leafy greens, like spinach, broccoli, kale, and other dark-green vegetables.

The biggest concentration of this nutrient is found in garnet amaranth, green basil, pea tendrils, and red cabbage. On the other hand, greens like popcorn, golden pea tendrils, magenta spinach, and red orach microgreens showed less than 0% of this compound.

Color seems to be a valid indicator of content, meaning that you can rely on your judgment to assume that the darker greens and bright reds are richer in this nutrient than light-oranges and yellows.

You don't have to be a scientist nor put each microplant under the microscope to conclude its dominant nutrient. If you're working to boost your blood circulation, this nutrient will give you exactly what you need.

The maturity of the plant also plays a vital role, meaning that grown varieties contain less of this nutrient than microgreens.

VITAMIN C

Vitamin C, or ascorbic acid, is an important antioxidant. However, to preserve vitamin C in microgreens, you'll have to protect them from stress and provide optimal, stable, and continuous conditions for healthy growth.

The varieties known to have the greatest amounts of vitamin C include garnet amaranth and red cabbage, with opal basil and china rose radish being runner-ups. In fact, the amount of vitamin C that was found in these plants was nearly double the amount found in mature species.

While this doesn't mean adult vegetables are useless, it shows how you can navigate food supplementation, like seasoning, juices, and smoothies, to boost the number of nutrients lacking in your regular diet.

If you find yourself lacking vitamin C yet hate eating cabbage, you can disguise it into a tasty smoothie by adding a small amount of the microgreen substitute.

CAROTENOIDS

Microgreens can become a potent source of carotenoids, like beta-carotene, also known as provitamin A. This essential nutrient has antioxidative properties, protecting cellular membranes of your body from passing through free radicals.

The words "antioxidant" and "free radicals' are often used when discussing cellular regeneration and cancer prevention, with antioxidants helping the body release toxic chemicals instead of absorbing them.

The microgreens found to be richest in this nutrient include red sorrel as the most substantial source, with cilantro, pepper cress, and red cabbage following closely. You'll find the least amount of beta-carotene in popcorn shoots and golden pea.

Compared to adult plants, the leading carotene microgreens contain anywhere from 10 to 260 times the nutrient levels. This only goes to show the abundance of the nutrient compared to adult plants and how much antioxidant benefits you can gain with only small dosages.

When it comes to the health of your eyesight, lutein and zeaxanthin are carotenoids that accumulate in the macula of your eyes, supporting healthy, sharp vision. In fact, they're believed to reduce the possibility of developing cataracts and prevent the degeneration of ocular tissues.

To boost your eyesight, you can grow cilantro, garnet amaranth, red cabbage, and red sorrel. Studies have shown that these microgreens contained significantly higher amounts of the eye-nurturing compound compared to adult specimens. The secret lies in the leaves of these plants, which seem to be most saturated with lutein.

Another carotenoid called violaxatine, which is an orange carotenoid, was found to be most concentrated in cilantro microgreens, with lush amounts of it present in other microgreens as well. Again, the amounts were highly abundant compared to grown plants.

POTENT
MICRONUTRIENTS

When it comes to researching the nutritional value of microgreens, it's been proven that micro elements and macro elements like potassium, calcium, iron, copper, sodium, manganese, phosphorus, magnesium, and zinc are all very high in all brassica microgreens.

While this varies based on varieties and species, the vitamin K, manganese, potassium, calcium, and phosphorus levels show the highest concentrations in wasabi microgreens, with the lowest value being in daikon radish microgreens.

The concentration of phosphorus and calcium was the highest in savoy cabbage and lowest in wheatgrass. Magnesium showed the highest values in microgreen cauliflower and lowest in red mustard. The concentration of sodium showed to be the greatest in watercress and lowest in ruby radish.

The levels of the important macro elements of phosphorus, calcium, potassium, and iron were also high in microgreens, showing that purple kohlrabi and red cabbage had the greatest concentrations of these nutrients, alongside zinc and copper. The majority of other microgreens were also very potent in these ingredients, which are considered to be of vital importance for maintaining a strong immune system.

On the other hand, grass microgreens had great amounts of manganese, while the least nutritious microgreens showed to be mustard, Chinese cabbage, red kale, and ruby radish. Typical commercial selling conditions didn't prove to affect the microgreens negatively, as the tested samples didn't contain any heavy metals.

If you are looking for true superfoods, research suggests that you should cultivate pea shoots, followed by kohlrabi, which also contains high amounts of valuable nutrients.

Red mustard seems to remain the least nutritive. However, it still had an abundant number of vitamins. One of the reasons why microgreens are so potent in nutrients is that, at this stage of growth, the plants accumulate numerous vitamins and minerals.

In fact, plants pile up vitamin K, phosphorus, and zinc, so that they can support their further growth functions. On the other hand, iron and calcium will be accumulated during more mature phases of growth when the micro green is ready to harvest.

TOCOPHEROL

This is a substance that qualifies under vitamin E. Vitamin E also includes the substance known as tocotrienol. These substances are soluble in fat. What research showed was that the most important types of substances in this category, like alpha-tocopherol and y-tocopherol, were abundant in microgreens.

They are most concentrated in green daikon radish, which was highly rich in both types of the substances. If you are aiming to boost your nutrition with vitamin E, you should aim to plant opal radish.

The lowest rated microgreens when it came to the saturation of this nutrient were golden pea tendrils. However, even this small plant contains more vitamin C than mature spinach leaves. Red cabbage microgreens are found to contain a large amount of vitamin E as well.

To sum up, microgreens contain enormous amounts of important nutrients that often range from 10 times to 200 times compared to adult green leaves and vegetables. Considerably higher amounts of keratinocytes and vitamins, compared to adults of the same plants, were found in their microversions. You'll find the greatest amounts of vitamins K and E in green daikon radish, cauliflower, amaranth, garnet, and red cabbage.

On the other hand, the lowest-rated microgreens, when it comes to concentrations of essential nutrients, include golden pea tendrils and popcorn shoots. However, these microgreens still contain large amounts of nutrients compared to fully grown vegetables.

This concentration severely reduces with insufficient light. It's been proven that, for example, gold pea tendrils lose a lot of vitamins and keratinocytes if they don't have enough light. If you're thinking about boosting your diet with microgreens, you need to be aware that their environment and conditions seriously impact the amount of nutrients that they will be able to synthesize.

Always keep in mind that the nutrients don't come from the plant itself but instead from the conditions that were provided.

When it came to commercially grown microgreens, the results were slightly different. Whether microgreens are grown for commercial purposes or for personal use made a lot of difference with the amount of vitamins they contained and desirable dietary intake. When cultivating microgreens for personal use, consider the fact that many conditions affect their nutrient density.

NUTRITIONAL BENEFITS OF MICROGREENS

It is beyond question that you can use microgreens to enrich your diet with healthy nutrients. As they are undoubtedly more saturated with nutrients compared to full-grown plants, they have proven to be highly beneficial for average users.

Flavor seems to be one of the biggest factors contributing to the general acceptance of microgreens. However, this greatly depends on quality of maintenance, which is best done with modified atmosphere packaging and keeping the plants at moderately low temperatures.

If the plants found in stores get exposed to direct light, their nutrient concentration will decay significantly and quickly. Forms of transportation and light exposure also contribute to faster decay of vitamins and other nutrients found in microgreens. There are other additional risks when it comes to commercial microgreen growing and shopping for the plants in grocery stores.

Some research revealed low-to-moderate contamination from *E. coli*. However, this risk is still smaller compared to sprouts.

One of the reasons why microgreens are more nutrient dense than mature plants can be explained by gene expression and biosynthesis during growth. It seems that microgreens process enzymes differently while the seeds are growing, which can have a great impact on their nutritional value.

When selling and purchasing ready-to-eat microgreens, it is important to note that postharvest storage and wash treatment need to be done in optimal conditions for good quality and prolonged shelf life. While there's little-to-no fresh microgreens appearing in stores, it is important to note that the way you wash and dry the plants, as well as how you package and sanitize them, can increase the risks of losing nutrients and contaminating the plants with different pathogens.

However, the majority of microgreens can be found as live plants, sold in grocery stores, and served in restaurants completely safely and without any consequences.

However, a great misconception about microgreens is that they will last longer because they're living plants. Note: a plant being sold alive, in its pot, doesn't guarantee long shelf life! Considering the fact that they need constant and moderate exposure to light to maintain their photosynthesis or else they wither; they can also lose a lot of their potency during transportation. This can negatively impact their nutritional quality and flavor. When it comes to the risks of developing germs, microgreens usually carry low risk of contamination by *E. coli* and other pathogens.

When looking into the nutritional value of microgreens, it is clear that they are far more abundant in all sorts of replenishing nutrients. You also have to understand that this doesn't diminish the importance of adult vegetables.

When thinking about the right species to grow, you should think about your own nutritional needs and preferences when it comes to taste. Microgreens are very sensitive to environmental influences, so it's important to think about what kind of conditions you can provide and whether the particular species aligns with your ability to take care of it properly.

There are many important microgreens that demand complete emulation of their natural conditions. For this reason, think about whether you can provide these conditions.

NUTRITIONAL VALUE OF INDIVIDUAL MICROGREENS

N ow, let's look into some individual properties of different microgreens. Types
known to be among the most beneficial
include:

- **Amaranth** is most suitable to grow either hydroponically or in soil. While it takes only about 12 days before you can harvest it, it will have a vibrant red or rose color. It tastes sweet and very fresh. It is also highly rich in beta-carotene, iron, calcium, and vitamins C and K.

- The next most popular microgreen is **Arugula**. This small plant doesn't need presoaking before planting, and you can choose any medium to grow it in. It develops quite fast, being able to reach the harvest stage after only eight days. It will be colored deep green and have a strong, peppery flavor that will resemble cabbage. Its stems are fresh and crisp, and the plant is rich in phosphorus, iron, calcium, and vitamin C. It is also a good plant to fight free radicals, as it contains many carotenoids and minerals such as calcium, manganese, and iron, which are all essential for a healthy diet.

- **Barley** usually grows after nine days, when you can harvest it and enjoy its sweet taste.

- **Basil** is another popular microgreen that grows in 12 days. However, it is ideal to harvest it after 10 days, as this is the time when it will have the most intense flavor and the highest amount of nutrients.

- **Beets** are highly rich in protein, zinc, iron, magnesium, calcium, potassium, and vitamins C, K, E, and B. This highly nutritive microgreen will take between 11 and 21 days to mature, and you should grow it in soil. It tastes somewhat earthy, but sweet, and can be compared to wheatgrass.

- **Broccoli** will mature after only 12 days and provide you a steady supply of phosphorus, calcium, and numerous vitamins. Since it grows fast and requires minimum maintenance, you can grow it both hydroponically and in soil. It is one of the healthiest microgreens to cultivate.

- **Brussels sprouts** are rich in fiber, folic acid, and vitamins C, K, and B. They taste similar to cabbage and broccoli, only slightly more bitter. You can grow them on any medium of your choosing. You will recognize that it is mature for harvest after its stems become purple or pink. Most likely, this will happen after 14 days. However, it is important to know that Brussels sprouts don't respond to warmth very well.

- **Buckwheat** is yet another super food that contains plenty of fiber, vitamins K, B, and C, as well as folic acid. It is another microgreen that is painless to grow, with a high germination rate. However, you will need to soak the seeds in cold water a day before planting.

- **Microgreen cabbage** is rich in beta-carotenes, iron, and vitamins A and C. It has a soft, fresh texture with a typical brassica flavor that resembles broccoli. Its leaves can be colored different shades of green, or even red and violet. You will find it in numerous variations. However, all of them are very easy to cultivate. The green varieties contain a substantial amount of beta-carotene, while the red ones are rich in vitamin C. In addition, these plants are highly decorative, and you can use them to refresh the ambience of your home.

- **Cauliflower** is rich in iron, beta-carotenes, and essential vitamins like C and E. It shares a crispy texture and light taste similar to broccoli. Its stems, when maturing, become a purple or pink shade, with deep-green tops. It will take only up to 14 days before you can enjoy this nutrient-dense microgreen

- **Chia** is another food that is known to be a genuine nutritional bomb when it comes to iron. It contains abundant amounts of this nutrient, and it will take only up to 10 days to harvest. Chia microgreens are also rich in proteins, amino acids, and omega oils. They have a soft, tangy flavor, and also a pleasant smell.

HEALTH EFFECTS

Health benefits of microgreens are one of the major reasons why they became so popular and well-accepted among those who care about their health and well-being. But, what are the true benefits from consuming microgreens?

IMPROVED
DIGESTION

Studies have found that microgreens offer great benefits when it comes to nutrient richness. In fact, they are abundant in fiber, which replenishes your digestive system, as well as vitamins and minerals essential to create, preserve, and regenerate cells and tissues inside the body.

Overall, these nutrients contribute to strengthening your immune system and preventing diseases. In addition, microgreens help you manage weight due to the high amount of fiber that improves digestion and high amount of nutrients that can make every diet nutritional regardless of the calorie count.

If you are dieting and trying to lose weight with microgreens, you will ingest a lot of nutritional value without growing your fat cells and creating the fat supplies that will frustrate you when stepping on the scale.

CELLULAR
REGENERATION

Perhaps, one of the most beneficial health benefits of microgreens is the antioxidant property. Microgreens are abundant in antioxidants, aside from vitamins and minerals.

While antioxidants help you eliminate the unstable molecules from your body, which is found to prevent cancer, vitamins found in these small plants support the essential physiological processes that boost your immune system, improve your mental abilities, and also affect beauty.

The antioxidant properties help you remove free radicals from your body. These substances result from the body's natural processes and numerous negative environmental influences.

Free radicals start to form in your body when you live in a polluted environment, eat foods that are saturated with unhealthy sugars and fats, consume a lot of alcohol, as well as when you smoke and drink a lot of caffeine. Free radicals are also linked to a stressful lifestyle, which results in increased amounts of cortisol secretion. While your body has a certain ability to remove these harmful substances, they can still accumulate when the body is overwhelmed with negative influences. Consuming nutrient-dense foods that contain antioxidants can help you get rid of these harmful chemicals.

While the exact antioxidant types depend on each plant, they are generally known to possess multiple types of these beneficial compounds, regardless of species.

For example, the microgreens that come from the brassica family, which includes broccoli, are rich in vitamin E, which is a phenolic antioxidant. On the other hand, keratinoid antioxidants are found in lettuce, chicory, and other asteraceae microgreens.

Still, exact details of how microgreens can prevent illnesses remains covered with a veil of secrecy, which scientists are working hard to uncover. Here are a couple more important scientific findings about the health benefits of microgreens.

KIDNEY DISEASE

If you have kidney disease, the microgreens that contain high levels of potassium, such as leafy microgreens, lettuce, and chicory, can be very beneficial. In addition, microgreens are a great solution for people who follow a vegan or vegetarian diet, as well as adding more fiber to their daily nutrient intake.

There's some evidence that these foods, since they don't require soil and can be grown in simulated environments, are even suitable for astronauts.

Sustainability is one of the major benefits of the cultivation of microgreens. As they don't require the same amount of labor as classic gardening, they can be a low-cost way to introduce healthy and beneficial foods into your daily life.

They are also appropriate for growing in confined spaces while maintaining the variety and bulk amounts of plants. They provide a consistent source of natural nutrients, as they require only a couple of weeks to grow enough to be consumed. In fact, by simply rotating a couple of selected species, you can have a new, fresh batch in your kitchen every single week.

CARDIOVASCULAR HEALTH

Microgreens have been found to potentially benefit those who cope with high blood pressure, cardiovascular disease, obesity, and diabetes. They can also help the healing of those who are recovering from stroke.

Sadly, these diseases, alongside cancer, are flourishing in developed countries due to poor work-life balance and insufficient time to rest and devote to health.

While a general recommendation is to consume a minimum of 400 grams of vegetables and fruits daily, as they are a rich source of micronutrients, antioxidants, and vitamins, insufficient exposure to the sun and a diet that consists of fat, processed sugars, and carbohydrates remain most prevalent among citizens in developed countries.

However, it is important to consider that improper handling of microgreens can cause a decline in flavor and nutritional value of crops, mainly affecting potatoes, and other tubers, as well as leafy greens and other horticultural crops. It is also important to consider that seasonal plants that are grown locally are much more saturated with nutrients than those that are imported.

When thinking about the nutritional value of microgreens by species, types of microgreens like legumes, and others that include soybean sprouts, and traditional ones like radish, mustard, and amaranth, contain substantially larger amounts of micronutrients compared to grown vegetables across the different stages of growth, from sprouts to microgreens, and then a fully grown plant.

One of the biggest benefits from microgreens comes from a high saturation of the so-called phytonutrients, which contribute to intense taste and flavor, while helping those with a deficiency of micronutrients.

This means that if you are deficient in vitamins like C, A, E, and K, or substances like keratin, beta-carotene, and potassium, you can avoid supplementation and instead use microgreens to compensate for the lacking nutrients, while reaping great benefits in flavor and taste.

Another benefit of these foods is that they can be consumed raw. You don't have to cook or prepare microgreens in any way, which would otherwise reduce their nutritional value.

Grown fruits and vegetables contain high amounts of nutrients. On most occasions, they need to be either processed or cooked, which further depletes them of beneficial substances.

You are free from having to cook microgreens, which means that you get to consume the highest amount of their potentially regenerative nutrients.

But, what are the advantages of home-grown microgreens?

Growing your microgreens on a windowsill or terrace by simply storing them in containers, with the possibility of growing numerous crop seeds, will give you fresh produce in 7 to 15 days. In addition, you won't have to use any fertilizers or pesticides to protect them from negative influences and possible infections, which means that you get to consume foods that are completely organic and free from toxic chemicals.

Compared to store-bought vegetables, which are most often treated with pesticides and require processing before you eat them, microgreens aren't depleted of nutrients, and they won't introduce any additional toxins into your body.

You can grow microgreens by first washing the seeds and soaking them in water for up to six hours. They need to be kept at room temperature.

After this, you only need to place them in a suitable container, which can be either a plastic tray, a plastic container, or a plate. You can also pack them into a glass jar or any other container of your choosing.

After that, you can simply cover them with a paper towel or a regular cloth, to preserve their moisture and optimal temperature. After this, you only need to rinse and sprinkle the seeds with water daily to support the sprouting process. You need to provide the seeds with drainage as well, which will keep bacteria or fungi from growing. For misting, it is best to use distilled or spring water.

It is important to remember that microgreens need nutrients for healthy growth. For this, you should use a soil substitute, or regular soil, whether organic or inorganic.

You can also use hydroponic nutrient film towels, which will help you easily pull out of the plant when it's time for harvesting. Another convenience of growing microgreens is that they need fewer seeds than growing sprouts.

In this chapter, you learned about the amazing nutrient saturation found in microgreens. You learned that they contain from a couple to ten times more nutrients than their grown versions, with some micros exceeding the adult varieties by over 200 times when it comes to nutritional value.

This served to prove the potency of these plants and their significance for a healthy diet. Moreover, you learned how and why microgreens become so potent. As you learned, they pile up, preserve, and contain nutrients to secure the next stage of growth. At the stage of a microgreen, a plant gathers all the nutrients needed to become a fully grown plant. This explains why it's essential to harvest at this exact stage, before the plant starts processing the nutrients and proceeds growing.

Moreover, you learned how exactly your health benefits from these amazing plants. If you're looking to simply boost your immune system, the abundance of vitamins, minerals, and other complex nutrients like beta-carotenes, tocopherols, and others, will make you germ proof, and will also contribute to sharp vision, a strong, vigorous heart, and sufficient iron in your blood.

In addition, if you're looking for support in recovery from illnesses like kidney disease or cancer, the antioxidants found in microgreens, in staggering amounts, will support your body in getting rid of free radicals, which are the substances that intervene with proper cell regeneration.

The cell-regenerating property of antioxidants is a topic on its own. You see, for your body to remain healthy and rejuvenated, the cells need the ability to process and get rid of their old, decaying parts. If their capacity to do this depletes, old and decaying cells remain in your system.

This is as bad as it sounds, as compromised cellular regeneration is associated with illnesses we'd rather not name, from allergies, weakened immune systems, and respiratory infections, to severe ones like autoimmune disease, cancer, lupus, and others.

Consume abundant antioxidants from microgreens, and you will support your body in metabolizing the dead, decaying, and flawed cells of your body, to fuel and support regeneration and the growth of new, healthy cells and tissues.

However, whether you're looking to grow at home or turn your hobby into a business, your journey begins with finding the best seeds. In the next chapter, we will present you with the right strategies for finding the best seeds to grow microgreens.

A quality microgreen requires more than care and environment. The quality of seeds comes first, as the seed carries the plant's genetic potential to produce, process, and synthesize nutrients.

Furthermore, the treatment and handling of seeds prior to planting also determines the health of the future plant. For this reason, the next chapter will give you the necessary instructions to first choose the varieties you want to grow, and then obtain the best quality seeds.

CHAPTER 3: HOW TO CHOOSE THE BEST SEEDS

In the previous chapter, you learned more about the nutritional benefits of microgreens. You learned that their reputation for being superfoods is firmly backed up by science and that their value goes beyond eye-pleasing and palate-delighting traits.

Microgreens are genuinely abundant in the majority of nutrients needed for proper body functioning, a robust immune system, and vigorous cellular replenishment. You learned that the regular use of microgreens can, indeed, help your body wash away toxins and contaminants, battle bacteria and viruses, and more importantly, support your own natural regeneration process (Choe, Yu, & Wang, 2018).

Now that you've decided to start cultivating these potent herbs, the first step is to choose the best quality seeds. The quality of your plant won't only depend on your care. The very basis of nutrient-dense microgreens is a potent seed, that has the right genetic makeup for vigorous growth and has been cared for to preserve the potential it carries.

The importance of quality seeds for microgreens is enormous. First things first, the seed quality mainly determines the germination rate. Simply put, this rate determines how many seeds will sprout and turn into growing plants.

A high germination rate means that the seeds are healthy, well-nourished, and genetically suitable to produce healthy plants. The seeds with a high germination rate mainly come from reputable, quality suppliers who pay attention to the way they collect, nurture, store, package, and transport seeds. While genetics is a major contributor to the quality of the seed, it's treatment can either preserve or deplete the seed of its capacity to grow.

On the other hand, suppliers who don't pay enough attention to the quality genetic selection of their crops and the treatment of their seeds tend to market seed packages with a low germination rate. A low germination rate essentially means that only a portion of planted seeds will sprout, and the quality of the plants that grow out of them is also questionable.

On the other hand, good germination capacity is also important to prevent contamination from mold, fungi, and bacteria. This particularly goes for micros like the tender amaranth, peas, and sunflower. These are only some of the plants that will wither with the barest appearance of pathogens, which will quickly infect and diminish the entire plate of growing crops. This can ruin your efforts and demotivate you from future cultivation, which is something I'd like to help you avoid.

In addition, quality seeds are GMO-free and organic, and I'll help you discover the right ways to obtain seeds that possess these two important traits. However, before you head off to purchase seeds, it would be wise to first decide on the crops to cultivate. We've created a short list of beginner-friendly microgreens, which you'll find in the following section.

DECIDE ON
DESIRED CROPS

Before deciding to start growing microgreens, it is important to first decide on the varieties you want to cultivate. For starters, it's important to note that you can choose any type of vegetable or herb you like and cultivate it as a microgreen.

In fact, you can pick up the seeds of any vegetable you enjoy, plant it properly, and then pluck it once it reaches the microgreen stage. While this is a simple philosophy, deciding on the plants you want needs some contemplation.

The first thing you want to consider is the taste. Which tastes do you prefer? Would you like to use your plants to simply add aroma to your cuisine, or do you want to eat greater amounts of them, in which case you'll focus on veggies you already enjoy?

Microgreens vary in taste and can give a mild,

spicy, sweet, bitter, or sour effect, depending on the species. The choice of flavors depends on what you usually prefer in your diet, minding the fact that some of the delicate greens vary not only in the type but also the intensity of the flavor.

With this in mind, here's a short overview of microgreens by family. This short list will help you narrow your choices and map out the possible winners for your future DIY kitchen garden. As you browse this list, keep in mind that the tastes are similar to those of adult plants and choose a couple to focus on for starters. You can group microgreens in different families that all encompass different types of varieties. While there are some differences in tastes and textures, usually the crops from the same family are similar. Here are a couple of most common microgreen crops, grouped by family:

- The **amaranthaceae** family includes quinoa, swiss chard, beets, spinach, and amaranth.
- Popular veggies like onions, chives, garlic, and leeks are a part of the **amaryllidaceae** family.
- Fennel, dill, celery, and carrots belong to the **apiaceae** family.
- The **asteraceae** family includes radicchio, lettuce, endive, and chicory.
- The **brassica** family includes watercress, radish, cauliflower, cabbage, broccoli, and arugula.

- Squashes, melons, and cucumbers are part of the **cucurbita** family.
- Oregano, sage, rosemary, basil, and mint —the herb flavors you enjoy when seasoning meals—belong to the **lamiaceae** family.
- If you want to grow grasses and cereals, which include wheatgrass, gold rice, corn, and barley, look for them under the **poaceae** family.

I didn't compile this list to simply sound smart by using Latin names. Knowing the common traits of each family will help you read packages and get further informed on cultivation techniques and supplements in other sources, which mainly apply to individual families rather than specific species.

Now that you have some insight into the microgreens you're most likely to love, I'll help you make a choice by giving some more technical information about individual plants belonging to these families. Following are some recommendations for the microgreens that are the most beneficial yet very simple to cultivate:

Kohlrabi is rarely used in an average kitchen; you may also know it under the name of cabbage turnip. As it's the same species as cabbage, you will use its roots rather than leaves. The microgreen version of this plant will take up to 12 days to grow. You will know that they are ready to harvest when their stems grow taller, and the green leaves have thrived. This plant will give your meals a pop of color and a mild turnip-cabbage-y flavor. They are also great for salads and sandwiches.

Clover microgreens grow simple and fast, and they only take up to 12 days. They have a sweet and mild flavor that is most intense when picked young. Additionally, they are abundant in calcium, zinc, iron, and magnesium.

Collards grow hydroponically and are slightly smaller and slower in growth compared to chives. It will take up to 12 days for them to grow, and they will feature a dark green color. They have the same taste intensity as the grown vegetables.

Kale is one of the healthiest plants known and is also considered to be a superfood. If you don't enjoy the taste and texture of the fully grown plant, the microgreen form of this vegetable will taste similar to lettuce, albeit milder and more tolerable.

Alfalfa is another of the hydroponic microgreens that won't require soil. To plant them, all you need to do is soak an ounce of seeds on a paper towel and cover them for between three and five days. After 8 to 12 days, you will notice dark green leaves that will be crunchy and have a mild flavor. They are great to diversify the taste of sandwiches and salads.

Wheatgrass is one of the simplest microgreens to

grow. It looks similar to regular grass; however, it is abundant in many vitamins and minerals. Sadly, the general consensus is that the taste of this herb isn't great. If you don't enjoy the taste of this healthy microgreen, you can add it to a smoothie or improve the flavor by adding sugar or honey.

Sorrel will taste sour/tart. It has a lemony flavor and takes 20 days to harvest. Red vein sorrel is the most popular variety of this plant and will look similar to spinach.

Basil. Growing micro basil is also very simple and convenient, and you will get to enjoy an intense flavor that will add a touch of the exotic and Mediterranean to your kitchen. You shouldn't presoak the seeds, but instead directly plant them into the soil and slightly mist until they are damp. It grows quite quickly, but it will require higher temperatures to grow healthy, which is why you should preferably plant it during the spring or summer months. You can choose between multiple types, like cinnamon basil or lemon basil. Each of these species taste different but very intense.

Mustard is a flavorsome microgreen that has a spicy taste and will enhance the taste of many dishes and salads. It grows very fast and will be ready to harvest in about 10 days. The young plants are quite resilient, and they won't lose any of their flavor or properties even if you leave them growing slightly longer.

Buckwheat also grows very fast, and you only need to soak the seeds in cold water and leave them up to 24 hours. After that, before planting, choose either a large cup or a broad tray. You will most likely be able to harvest it within 12 days, after its yellow leaves start turning green. However, this plant will need a lot of light, meaning that you'll either keep it on your windowsill or add supplemental light for bulk cultivation.

Amaranth will grow and spread out after 12 days, when you will be able to harvest it. You can keep it safely in the refrigerator, and it will maintain its flavor for a long time. It should be intensely red and have slender leaves. These microplants are most often used for garnishes.

Sunflower is yet another superfood that will take only up to 4 days to produce green leaves that will make a great addition to any salad or sandwich.

Peas will require sufficient water, as they absorb substantial amounts. After transferring soaked seeds (preferably after 24 hours of hydration) into a ball or a tray, mist them multiple times a day until you notice sprouting. After that, you can transfer them into soil, using around 12 oz of seeds per tray. After you've planted the sprouts, keep them out of light between three and five days, but proceed with misting. The soil needs to be just dampened; otherwise, the plants might get soggy. The peas will take around 12 days before you can harvest them and enjoy their sweet and crunchy taste.

Microgreen **carrots** taste similar to regular carrots, only sweeter, finer, and softer. However, it will take them around four weeks before harvesting. They will be worth the effort, considering they will be highly saturated with beta-carotene and vitamins C, E, and D.

Arugula has a spicy, peppery flavor that will give some flair to your sandwiches and salads. You can harvest in only seven days, as it only takes a couple of days to germinate.

Cress is great for those who are just starting out and can be grown either in soil or on a paper towel. However, you need to take good care of it and handle it gently, as it can easily bruise.

Now, you are free to decide which microgreens you want to plant! We recommend choosing between three and five if you're a beginner, preferably those with similar harvesting times and germination requirements. This will allow planting multiple species using similar techniques and tools, as well as simultaneous harvesting. However, if you're eager to learn, you can always combine the species to diversify tastes and flavors, while learning different techniques.

PURCHASE THE
BEST SEEDS

Now that you've decided which micro-greens you want to grow, it is also important to choose top-quality seeds. At the beginning of this chapter, we already highlighted the importance of high-quality seeds. Now, we'll present you with a couple of tips for finding the best seeds for your microgreens.

ORGANIC

It is very important that your seeds are untreated and organic. Purchasing seeds that are purposefully cultivated for sprouts and microgreens most likely means they were not treated with any chemicals like fungicides and pesticides.

On the other hand, if you're using gardening seeds, it is likely that they were treated with insecticides and fungicides. If your seed is treated with chemicals, the toxic chemicals will also remain in the plant, compromising its growth and nutritional value. Make sure to get only untreated seeds, whether you are ordering them online or purchasing from farmers' markets. Organically grown seeds are a bit harder to find but worth the trouble. It is also important to distinguish untreated from organic seeds.

While purchasing organic seeds means that they are not treated, buying specifically untreated seeds doesn't guarantee that they are organic. This means that the only guarantee of an organic seed is the certification you'll find on the packaging. This is the only way to secure top-quality seed. If you're unsure of whether a seed is organic, untreated, and GMO-free, ask the provider directly.

FIND A TRUSTED
SUPPLIER

Purchasing seeds from the cheapest online store is not going to be the wisest decision. Not only will you be unaware of the exact species and the quality of seeds that you will receive, there's also no guarantee that your seeds will be healthy and quality enough to grow. Make sure to research wisely, and pay attention to harvesting dates, as well as the provider's claims on seed longevity. Make sure to pay attention to the germination rates as well, as they suggest how many plants will sprout and grow.

GO FOR A LIMITED VARIETY

For starters, you don't want to stretch your efforts to an overly broad number of varieties. Instead, get to know each of the species that spark your interest, and find out what is best suitable for you. Beginners are usually successful with cultivating the popular brassica family, which can be demanding but worth the effort. This family includes turnip, broccoli, and cabbage. Another easy choice is mustard, which is flavorsome and quick and easy to grow. You'll also find lettuce, cress, sesame, bok choy, and Chinese cabbage to be beginner friendly.

PURCHASE FROM BULK SELLERS

As your confidence in your ability to grow microgreens strengthens, you can move on to buying seeds by ounces and pounds. Once you start cultivating larger amounts, it's recommended that you buy from bulk sellers, as they usually offer the best prices.

TAKE GOOD CARE
OF THE SEEDS

The quality and result of the seeds you purchase don't only depend on the supplier. They also depend on how much you care for the seeds. Taking good care of the seeds requires refrigerating them and protecting them from high temperatures, moisture, and air.

They also require cold temperatures and low humidity to be stored long term. Temperature fluctuations can promote germination and cause your seeds to sprout before time. On the other hand, refrigeration will keep them fresh for a very long time.

Also, keep in mind that the paper envelopes that serve to deliver the seeds won't be enough protection in the long run. You should remove them from their packaging and transfer them into watertight, but not completely airtight, plastic bags or clamp bags.

Alternatively, you can also keep the seeds in glass jars. Keep in mind that, while the seeds are in a dormant state, they are still living organisms that require care with due knowledge and responsibility. If you take care of them well, they will sprout with high germination rates, and grow as beautiful, potent, flavorsome plants as intended.

In this chapter, you learned how to pick, choose, and select the best species and seeds for your future collection. First, you learned the abundance of greens to choose from. With the liberty to grow as many types as you like, we suggested that you choose those you're most likely to enjoy and use, all while focusing to present you with the crops that are easiest to plant and grow. With this in mind, you've probably narrowed down your list to your top five.

After that, we suggested the right ways to obtain quality seeds. It is important to approach micro-green seed selection with great attention, as not only the quality of supply but also the way you care for the seeds determine their germination and the success of your batch. Care for the seeds is a shared responsibility between the supplier and you, meaning that you need to protect the seeds from temperature fluctuations and excess moisture while keeping them away from sunlight.

For this, it's recommended to keep the seeds refrigerated, preferably in glass jars. Now that you know which greens you want to grow and how to find the best seeds, it's time for you to learn the exact technique of growing, harvesting, and storing microgreens. We will cover this topic in the next chapter, giving you the exact steps to take for growing lush batches of greens.

CHAPTER 4:
HOW TO GROW
MICROGREENS

I n the previous chapter, you learned how to choose the crops that will fit your needs best. You can make your choice depending on taste, preference, ease of growth, and health needs. Whichever choice you made, now's the time to finally learn how to grow microgreens. After all, this is the most important part of the process.

While simple and easy, proper growing technique will make the process effortless if you follow these simple guidelines and adjust your approach to individual properties of the varieties you chose. For that reason, this chapter will show which exact crops require particular environments and circumstances to thrive.

The proper choice of the crops and seeds should yield maximum germination, ensuring that the greatest number of seeds planted develops into sprouts. For this, a careful choice of seed will provide a healthy genetic base, while your efforts to care for the growing plant will support it in transforming soil, water, and light into valuable nutrients.

In this chapter, you'll learn the exact steps needed to grow microgreens. It's essential to follow these steps religiously, as they create the proper conditions for the plant to grow. First, you will find out what tools and supplies are needed for cultivation of microgreens.

You'll find the list to be quite simple, mainly containing items you likely already have at home. However, steps need to be taken to prepare these tools to minimize the chances of contamination and trauma to the plants (Di Gioia et al., 2015).

Next, you'll find out how to properly germinate and plant the seeds. Individual varieties require different treatment for best germination. Most often, the seeds are hydrated with filtered water. However, some crops, as you'll learn, don't require soaking prior to germination, and these are usually the simplest to grow.

Finally, you'll learn about other important considerations relevant to growing a healthy batch. In this chapter, you'll learn about optimal temperature, lighting, storage, and harvesting processes recommended for highest yield.

You'll also learn about possibilities to further en-hance the potency of your plants with proper drainage, hydration, and fertilization. Bear in mind that general recommendations state that microgreens don't require additional supplemen-tation.

However, I encountered some evidence that shows that proper supplementation can, indeed, benefit the nutritional potency of particular microgreens. You may, if you want to, follow fer-tilization and supplementation advice, keeping in mind it's not a must for growing healthy crops. Now, it's time to start gathering tools and supplies for planting your first batches!

TOOLS AND SUPPLIES

One of the reasons why microgreens are so compelling to grow is the short amount of time that passes from sprouting to being harvested. They aren't a big investment, considering the benefits of having a fresh supply throughout the entire year.

Before you start growing your own microgreens, it is important to prepare and get all the supplies you will need. First things first, you will choose the exact variety you want to cultivate.

There are dozens of plants that you can grow as microgreens, but you should start with the one that is easiest to cultivate. We suggest starting off with the simplest microgreens, for example, sprouts, arugula, broccoli, cabbage, bok choy, cauliflower, chia, and Chinese mustard. You can also go for kale, as it is a plant that is relatively easy to cultivate. For starters, you want to select the best media to grow your microgreens in.

First things first, purchase only the amount of seed you will need for the first planting. As you already know, seeds can grow stale and get contaminated under the influence of bacteria and mold.

To prevent this, purchase only the smallest amounts for starters, and move to bulk seed purchasing once you gain more experience. Now, it's time to list the basic supplies your greens will need to grow and thrive.

CONTAINERS

After you've decided on the varieties to grow and purchased quality seeds, the next thing to think about is where you will store your microgreens. You can use anything from a specially built shed to a windowsill or even your kitchen counter.

However, you need a clean container; this can be in the form of a regular plastic container or a disposable pie plate. You can also go for salad bowls, fruit boxes, regular plates, or even plastic plates for hydroponically grown microgreens.

Since these DIY microgreen containers aren't made for these purposes specifically, you'll also have to think about drainage and pierce or drill holes across the bottom of the dishes so that the soil can release any excess water.

While you can use Tupperware, glasses, glass jars, etc., for more serious cultivation, you'll need microgreen trays. These containers are best to grow healthy microgreens, as they're made for these specific purposes. Whether or not you'll need to drill drainage holes depends on the substrate. If you're using hydroponically grown seeds, you won't need holes, particularly if you're using growth mats. However, soil media will require holes, since the excess water needs to be drained from the tray.

First things first, check all of the instructions, and follow the advice you find attached to products you purchase. Rely on the manufacturer's knowledge of best use, and stick to their suggestions for how to best use the products. Whether it's a container, lighting, soil, or any other piece of equipment, following instructions will ensure that the product performs at its best.

Later, when you're more experienced, you can add your own touch of creativity according to the knowledge of what works best.

WATER

The quality of hydration greatly determines the health, flavor intensity, and nutrient density of your crops. You'll preferably use either rainwater or a water filter, since regular tap isn't a good choice due to high pH value. When it comes to watering, you want to pay attention to the pH values of water and presoak the seeds that require doing so. Soaking will most likely be necessary for plants like buckwheat, beets, sunflower, popcorn shoots, and others. Tap water is usually too high in pH value for microgreens to process. You should get a pH test kit that ranges from pH two to pH eight. Ideally, you will provide water that has a pH value of six for watering your plants.

GROWTH MEDIA

We already discussed choosing between hydroponic growth pads, soil-less, and soil media. This choice mainly depends on the type of microgreen, with some room to adjust the mix to your own preference.

There are multiple types of growth media to choose from, ranging from soil based to soil-less and hydroponic:

The soil-based mediums will require a planting mix that will drain well. The mix shouldn't contain any stones or clumps. Instead, it should be light and compact. Preferably, you will add nutrients through hydration, keeping in mind not to go overboard. The soil can start developing microbes if it is too wet. You can use soil to grow many greens, including basil. But, keep in mind that soil isn't the best choice for all of them.

The media that don't include soil are made from different mixes like perlite, vermiculite, and coco coir. You can also use organic clay pebbles or hydroponic lava. One of the bigger advantages of this medium is that you can adjust and level it to give a clean surface. This will be important when you start to harvest, as the plants are harvested close to the soil. It will also provide a clean surface that won't spread a lot of dirt.

Using hydroponic methods is very simple and easy for beginners. Hydroponic medium consists of a growth pad, which you will use to retain water and allow the seed to absorb it. This method will also enable germination, allowing the seed to sprout while staying continuously hydrated. If you do this properly, you will have crops that are easy to harvest without having to pull them out.

Keep in mind that the choice of the medium doesn't only depend on your taste. It also depends on the type of the plant. With microgreens, you won't need fertilizer. However, if you still desire to use it, we recommend getting specialized fertilizers that are tailored to fit the individual needs of particular varieties you're cultivating.

ILLUMINATION

Besides your growth medium, lighting deserves some attention. We already discussed the illumination needed for microgreens to grow healthy. However, if the place you're storing them in supplies sufficient light, you don't have to think about adding supplemental illumination. However, if you estimate that your plants might need a boost of photons, or you grow them on racks, you can start looking into the alternatives for LED illumination, depending on your needs and budget. After you've planted your microgreens, you will wait an estimated amount of time for them to grow, after which you can move on to harvesting.

In this section, you learned about all supplies needed for successful microgreen cultivation. Once you start the process yourself, keep in mind that the advice given varies by individual species and varieties. Upon choosing a couple of plants to start with, choose those tools and methods that are the best fit for the variety in question. In the next section, you'll learn the exact steps needed to successfully grow microgreens.

THE PROCESS
OF GROWING
MICROGREENS

N ow that you've gathered all of the supplies, the time has finally come to plant
your seeds. The following section will
give you precise steps and advice to successfully
plant the chosen seeds and care for them until
they flourish into microplants.

HOW TO PLANT MICROGREENS

Here's a step-by-step guide for planting microgreens.

Prepare the Container

After receiving and presoaking the seeds (if applicable), you will prepare your container. The first step is to carefully read the instructions that came with the seed package.

Check all of the instructions, and follow any advice and recommendations given. Read through the instructions carefully and check to see what advice the manufacturer gives regarding hydration and watering, drainage, placement, and other necessary actions to take good care of the growing plant.

When it comes to preparing your trays, you'll have to drill small holes into the bottom, so that plants can dispose of excess water. Of course, you won't have to do this if the trays or storage boxes you purchased already contain drainage holes. Ideally, your trays and storage boxes will measure roughly 10" x20", which is a standard measurement that applies to instructions on planting and dosing the seeds. Choosing trays of standard size will ensure effortless work going forward, as you won't have to do further calculations to adjust hydration, lighting, and temperature.

Add Soil/Growing Medium

The soil should be loose and scattered so that the seeds can have enough air. First, you will cover the bottom of your container with the substrate, or soil, that you intend to plant. It should be a thin layer of only an inch or two of soil, which should be moist but not soaked. You should level and flatten the soil but not press it completely so that it becomes hard.

Plant the Seeds

Next, it's time to insert the seeds. You should scatter them evenly across the soil, and then press gently using a piece of cardboard or your hands. The goal is for the seeds to be sufficiently covered with soil but not so overly pressed as to deprive them of oxygen. The next step is to cover the seeds with another thin layer of soil, keeping in mind that this layer should be loose, again, for the purposes of allowing your future plants to breed.

Light or Blackout?

The next step is to set-up the light. How you man-age the light and illuminate your microgreens greatly affects their growth and nutrient richness. The first few days after planting the seeds is the so-called stacking period, which will last throughout four to five days after seeding. The germinating process will require humidity and a lot of hydra-tion. However, during this time, you want to keep the seeds away from light.

You can do this by using a blackout dome, which is essentially a tray that you can flip over the seeds. You will have to mist the seeds and the lid at least twice a day to keep a moderate amount of humid-ity. However, not all seeds require blackouts, so take this step only if required.

After four or five days, your plants will be ready to be exposed to light, and with some crops, you can strengthen their roots by flipping over the blackout dome and allowing it to sit on top of the emerging crop for at least a day. Whether you will use supplemental lighting depends on the natural light of the room.

If there's enough light in the room where you keep your microgreens, you won't need supplemental light. Different species will also vary in their il-lumination requirements. Study each individual species before making this decision.

If the crop that is emerging looks pale and soggy, it means that it needs more light. If you are growing using stack racks, you will need supplemental light because racks themselves will create shade.

Mist and Water

You will then mist and dampen the soil and cover the container using plastic wrap or the lid that might come with the container. Your container should remain covered until you notice sprouts. While waiting to see the sprouts, you should mist the container, up to twice a day. However, neither the container nor the soil should be too wet.

When you notice that the seeds have started sprouting, you can then remove the cover and proceed with daily misting as recommended. After this, you will wait a couple of days, preferably for four days, for your microgreens to thrive in direct sunlight.

If you are growing them in winter, they may need some supplemental lighting. If the plants become pale, it means that they are not getting enough illumination, in which case you can use supplemental lighting.

HOW TO HARVEST MICROGREENS

There's nothing overly complex or difficult about harvesting. You need a sharp tool to cut as close to the bottom of the plant as possible. Some of the plants can be easily pulled out, after which you should trim off the base and roots. After this, you'll spread them around to check if any of them still have seeds, keeping in mind to remove remaining impurities, like soil.

You can wash the greens if you plan on eating them right away but not if you plan on storing them. Before serving the plants, make sure to remove as much water as possible using a salad spinner. Some plants can spend some time on paper towels to dry, while others whither within minutes and need to be consumed right away.

Keep in mind that each variety demands different postharvest treatment. They are fragile to various degrees, and you want to make sure not to handle them too harshly or else they might wither and turn to mush.

However, a lack of due attention might cause your efforts to fail. Misting, watering, and paying attention to harvesting times is all necessary for quality produce.

For starters, you can choose between different herbs, leafy vegetables, and salad greens. You can grow a wide range of microgreens, including edible flowers. However, beginners do best with cultivating one type of seed and then moving on to a broader range of varieties, as they get to know the process.

Usually, this is either buckwheat, sunflower, mustard, cabbage, or cauliflower. These are among the simplest microgreens to grow as they require very little work and can be grown in a single container.

However, you can also grow them in different containers. You can take up a different approach with choosing your seeds by determining your dietary needs. Some microgreens are best suited for salads and sandwiches, for example, and you can start by determining which flavors and nutrients you want and make your decision like that.

You can also think about the color. Microgreens can come in a variety of shades, from deep green to intense purple and red. Also, keep in mind to think about your climate and the conditions you have for supplemental lighting and heating. Preferably, you'll choose those microgreens that don't require many environmental adjustments and can be grown in the garden.

They will be pretty simple to plant and cultivate. However, those species that are fragile and require LED lighting and protection from weather conditions may easily succumb to environmental influences if you don't have enough time or resources to devote to their care and maintenance. Usually, microgreens are very simple to cultivate.

However, many people don't have enough time in their day to devote to their care. If your day is busy and you can't spend too much time tending to your greens, it is best to choose those crops that require minimum maintenance.

The next thing to think about is where you will store your microgreens. Depending on the size of your batch, you'll store them either in your own refrigerator or a specialized appliance. Typically, small produce requires a small space, while larger-scale produce will require additional space and appliances.

IMPORTANT CONSIDERATIONS (SAFETY, HYGIENE, FERTILIZING, ETC.)

QUALITY OF LIGHTING

For supplementing lighting, you can use four- or eight-inch LED bars for each shelf or microgreen tray. LED lights will give enough illumination to meet the needs of the microgreens and come in a variety of prices, sizes, and shapes. To begin with, you can use shop lights. If you already have them at home, you can attach LED bulbs combined with incandescent light, while being thoughtful of lighting requirements for the plants you're growing. Most microgreens grow well at room temperature. You can get the exact information about temperature requirements from the seed supplier.

HARVEST AND POSTHARVEST FACTORS

There are many preharvest factors that affect the quality of microgreens. The selection of species, among the commercial cultivators, is greatly determined by the popularity of individual varieties.

Considering the enormous variety of microgreens when it comes to production, it's noted that the brassica family is the most user friendly and the most popular genotype for cultivating. It is popular due to its intense flavor, texture, appearance, and chemical composition.

Nutritional value is another important factor that contributes to the popularity of this variety. When measuring the total 25 genotypes, across 19 different species, in terms of the concentration of essential nutrients, the results showed great variability when it came to content of vitamins and nutrients under the great influence of different conditions. There was also a lot of variation when it came to micro elements and macro elements. These differences mainly apply to buckwheat, brassicas, and other varieties sensitive to environmental conditions.

Proper cultivation environment also seemed to affect the plant's antioxidant properties. Additional screenings were done on amaranth, which showed differences depending on harvesting status. The application of proper cultivation practices greatly affected nutritional value of the crops, with major differences found in broccoli crops, in terms of phenolic and flavonoid content.

Microgreens create an innovation in modern cooking specifically because of the popularity among consumers, with six species proving to be the most prominent when it comes to eating quality, texture, flavor, appearance, sweetness, sourness, and the abundance of tastes.

The brassica vegetables usually share flavors such as sour, bitter, and astringent, involving species like mustard grass and radish, which proved to be the least popular among consumers. The same can be said for the sweeter and colorful microgreens such as amaranth and beet. These foods have proven to be highly functional in providing high concentrations of phytonutrients and bioactive content, which is another important aspect of nutritional value when it comes to microgreens.

The same was concluded for pepper cress and red cabbage, as well as cilantro and amaranth. However, these greens share intense tastes, which may or may not align well with the preferences of users.

Research showed that sufficient amounts of photosynthetic photons, the particle that is emitted through supplemental illumination, is necessary to provide the microgreen with the conditions for photosynthetic processes.

An optimal level of lighting is necessary to provide both proper biological conditions and growth for economic purposes. Proper lighting will enable the plant to synthesize pigments, form leaves, and grow biomass. It's been proven that insufficient light interferes with healthy growth of the plant, resulting in hypocotyl elongation, and reduced leaf size and dried weight of the plant. On the other hand, proper lighting enhances the growth of different greens.

Species like bok choy and tatsoi grew healthiest under high LED lighting, which increases their sugar levels. Sugars are essential for the plant to grow and also improve the amount of pigmentation, particularly chloroplast pigments.

On the other hand, plants like lettuce grow healthiest under moderate LED light. A general consideration is that low levels of light reduce the amounts of chlorophyll in the plants, depriving them of one of the most beneficial compounds known to be able to rejuvenate and regenerate the human body. On the other hand, optimal lighting increases the development of this chemical, improving their antioxidant properties and yielding better biomass growth.

It's recommended to use higher lighting when growing brassica microgreens as well, as this improves their nutritional properties. The recommendation is to use an amount of light measuring over 400 μmol m^{-2} s^{-1} (the number of photons in a certain waveband incident over unit of time on a unit of area).

When plants find themselves under stress due to insufficient lighting, they tend to release antioxidants. This is unfortunate, as we want them to preserve these cell-regenerating substances. However, improving lighting reduces this response.

One of the most important aspects of providing microgreens with appropriate lighting is a possible impact on their growth and nutritional value. If you plan on cultivating microgreens at home, giving them a proper amount of light will take some learning, as not all species respond to LED lighting the same way. It's been found that the happy medium, when it comes to illuminating microgreens, ranges between 320 and 440 μmol m^{-2} s^{-1}. This is the light intensity range that shows to yield the best results, provided that other environmental elements, such as soil, temperature, and the quality of air, are kept within the same optimal measures.

Maintaining a moderate amount of light is the best recommendation when it comes to microgreens, as too intense light is proven to alter their antioxidant responses, without enhancing growth or nutritional value. You'll best support the plants by supplying a steady source of even, moderate light that will keep the plant's naturally occurring chemical processes in balance.

When it comes to the dry weight of the plants, it's been shown that commercially sold microgreens range from 4.6 to 10.2%. Analyzed by species, pea tendrils lead in dry weight percentage, with red beet containing over 90% of water.

NUTRITION/
SUPPLEMENTATION

When it comes to nutrition and biofortification, it was proven that microgreens require a proper amount of nutrients so that they produce high yields and premium quality. The growing medium plays a substantial role here, with supplementation and fertilization before sowing having a major impact on the nutrients that will later be synthesized in the plant.

Postharvest fertilization and presowing practices reportedly improve growth quality of these small plants. When it comes to fertilization, it is technically not necessary to produce good quality plants. However, it was proven to impact arugula and some other plants that respond well to additional nutrition.

Fertilizers that are recommended include ammonium nitrate, which has shown to enhance the growth of these plants as well as improve their photosynthetic responses and their chloroplasts. However, some species can accumulate nitrates, which can then be considered an unfriendly factor that can reduce their taste and nutritional value.

The application of fertilization seems to enhance the growth of microgreens. Different practices can be used to adjust the content of minerals and reduce the amounts of antinutrients that the plant will absorb, which will then improve its taste and extend shelf life. The degree to which the plants are able to accumulate minerals depends on species and the genotype.

If you're interested in profiting from microgreens, you can contact restaurants or people who might be interested in purchasing from you.

The most popular commercial microgreens include kale, broccoli, and arugula, which make for delicious salads. If you're interested in how to price your produce, you can always browse local stores and suppliers to see how much they charge for their products. An important factor to consider here is that you're producing fresh microgreens, that are far richer in flavor than those that have been refrigerated.

CHAPTER 5: HOW TO PREPARE AND CONSUME MICROGREENS

I n the previous chapter, you learned how to properly cultivate and harvest microgreens. However, you are doing all of it for the purpose of eating well and enriching your diet. For this, it is important to know how to properly take care of your plants after you've harvested them and how to properly use them in your diet.

While microgreens are nutrient dense, they are very sensitive to environmental conditions that can easily deplete them of their precious nutrients. For this reason, this chapter will give you more detailed instructions on how to not only store but also eat microgreens the right way.

First things first, we will briefly discuss storing microgreens after harvesting to preserve their freshness, flavor, and nutrients. Chances are that you won't eat the entire batch of your produce after they've matured. This is why you should only harvest and store the amounts you plan on using right away. It is usual for people to harvest the entire tray and then refrigerate the remainder of the plants.

However, this is not the best way to preserve nutrients, since these crops are highly perishable and will lose nutrients fast after they've been harvested. To preserve the maximum nutrients, it is important to either eat them fresh right away or store them properly. Before harvesting microgreens, it is important to have a precise, sharp tool. Preferably, you will use ceramic scissors or a ceramic knife. Ceramic is a nontoxic substance that is very light and gentle and won't chemically react with the nutrients in the greens.

The same can be said for metals. For example, if you use an old, rusty knife, it can contaminate your herb and reduce its nutritional value. Additionally, iron can transfer ions into the plant, which can accelerate the process of oxidation.

After this, the plants might brown and lose their flavor and nourishing properties. It is also important to sterilize your growing trays after harvest to remove any biofilm or other contaminants that can appear during the growing phase. Use soap and water and scrub the trays with a brush, cloth, or pressurized water. Then you can rinse the trays with water and spray with a 3% peroxide solution or 5-10% vinegar solution or wash in a bleach solution. Then rinse thoroughly and dry prior to your next use.

Another important thing to consider is to moisturize and allow air to flow through the plants. This means that you shouldn't store microgreens in sealed bags.

This will completely deplete them of air, and they will spoil and degrade quicker in these conditions. Instead, provide them with sufficient moisture and air flow. While you prepare your supplies for storing, you should lay out the produce onto a piece of paper towel or keep them in a container closet.

One you store the microgreens, they should be sheltered from exposure to light, which can further deplete them of nutrients. If you won't be eating your crops fresh, you should keep them in shade and protected from direct light. When properly refrigerated, microgreens will keep their freshness for about a week.

However, it is important to maintain the temperature of the refrigerator to 40 Fahrenheit, or roughly four degrees Celsius. You should never put microgreens in a freezer. In fact, some studies found that microgreens that are refrigerated at around 40 degrees Fahrenheit can last up to 21 days, while a warmer temperature reduces this time to up to 14 days.

However, this greatly depends on the variety, meaning that some will last longer than others. Keep in mind that the daily use of a refrigerator and opening it will briefly change the temperature. To check if your plants are doing well, keep an eye on how stored plants look. If they start to fade, become brown, or start to smell strangely, throw them out. This might be a sign that they've either started to rot or have grown moldy.

However, many users consider that microgreens can be well-preserved using plastic containers as well. While there's a variety of methods you can use to store microgreens, like plastic bags, plastic containers tend to prolong their shelf life.

Clamshell types seem to produce the best results. Usually, microgreens will stay fresh up to one week in clamshells. But, it is possible for this time to expand to two or more weeks depending on temperature, moisture, and each individual variety.

While bags are also useful for preservation, they come with a risk of developing mold, since it's a lot easier for moisture to condensate around the plants and create the environment for microbes to grow. On the other hand, clamshells will shelter your microgreens from being squashed and provide them with enough space and air.

If you close the clamshells properly and keep the

containers sealed, you will greatly extend the life-span and freshness of your plants. On the other hand, glass containers have proven ineffective in preserving the gentle baby plants.

For this, it is important for the containers to be sterilized. However, they will still increase condensation, which can affect the quality of your microplants. The possibility of condensation also means a fertile ground for mold and bacteria. In addition, glass containers tend to deplete the plants of taste and smell while preserving freshness. It is also important to be mindful of using single-use plastic and Tupperware as well.

While these containers can preserve freshness up to two weeks, it is possible for their quality to start to decline.

Another important thing to consider is to find the right place in your refrigerator when storing. Not all areas of the fridge have the same temperature. For example, if you put them on the top near the freezer, the low temperature can even freeze the plants.

It is important to keep them away from the cooling vent, which is the place where the temperature will most often fluctuate. Preferably, store them on the lower shelves of your refrigerator. You should also pay attention to the humidity of your refrigerator. Pay attention to whether there is condensation and moisture surrounding your plants, because this can degrade their quality.

On the other hand, the surroundings shouldn't be overly dry either. Since there's not much you can do to modify your refrigerator for storing microgreens properly, you can always cover them with a paper towel, which will pass air but maintain adequate moisture. Last but not least, you should be mindful of different varieties. The quality of seeds and conditions they were grown in and the way they were harvested all affect how long your microgreens will last, how fresh they will stay, and how rich they are in nutrients.

If stored properly, your microgreens will last between two or three weeks. However, since this highly depends on each individual crop, the best way to determine how long you can refrigerate each individual species is to study the crop itself.

HOW TO INCORPORATE MICROGREENS INTO YOUR DAILY DIET

When it comes to implementing microgreens properly into your diet, you should consider that finding the right ways to consume them affects the nutritional benefits that you will receive. The simple fact that these plants are nutrient dense doesn't guarantee good results unless you consume them properly.

While all studies confirm that microgreens are essentially nutrient bombs and calling them super foods is quite justified, benefiting from their high antioxidant content will require making them a part of your daily diet diligently and consistently.

Doing so will boost your immunity and reduce risks from heart disease, diabetes, obesity, and high blood pressure. However, if you don't stay regular when it comes to consuming microgreens, it is possible that you will miss seeing any particular results. Daily use is extremely important considering how easy and cheap it is to grow these plants at home. Here are a couple of ways to introduce microgreens into your daily diet.

SALADS

The first recommendation is to eat microgreens fresh in salads. Microgreens are healthiest when they are eaten raw. The less you process them, the more nutrients that are preserved. Their delicate flavors will also remain potent if you eat them right after harvesting. Cooking microgreens will deplete them of nutrients, which means that coming up with creative raw recipes is the right way to go. For example, the sunflower shoot, a small lemony-green plant, is a perfect addition to every salad.

WRAPS AND SANDWICHES

Next, you can make sandwiches and wraps using the freshly plucked herbs. You can use them to create intense, sweet, spicy, and overall fabulous flavors that will pack your meal with nutrients. For this, radish greens are usually the best condiments as they tend to go well with other fresh vegetables and meats.

While fresh microgreens will add some spiciness to your sandwiches and wraps, you should keep these recipes light and diet friendly, focusing on vegetables and greens instead of bread, meats, and toppings.

COOKED MEALS

You can also cook with microgreens. There are many types of microgreens that retain a lot of nutrients even when cooked. However, keep in mind that the best recommendation is to pop them into the dish at the very end of cooking and not allow them to be exposed to high temperatures for longer than a minute. Since these plants are perfectly safe to eat raw, and cooking doesn't do anything to intensify the flavor, you can even think about adding raw microgreens to already finished dishes. They are good to combine with fried dishes, pastas, and as side dishes.

JUICES AND SMOOTHIES

Another way to eat microgreens is to use them to create juices and smoothies. If you aren't a fan of eating raw plants, juices and smoothies are an easy way to incorporate them into your daily diet. For these purposes, wheatgrass has proven to be the most popular. If you add microgreens to a mixture of your favorite leafy greens, vegetables, and fruits in smoothies, they will add a touch of an individual flavor you enjoy. You can also create juices from microgreens on their own.

Keep in mind that you will need one part plants to three parts of water to create a refreshing drink that will contain enough nutrients.

COOKING GUIDE
FOR BEST NUTRIENT
PRESERVATION

One of the questions that's perpetually asked is whether or not microgreens are truly safe to eat raw. Generally, it is considered that raw microgreens are perfectly safe for daily use. However, removing the germs before eating is very important to eliminate the possibility of contracting fungus, parasites, bacteria, and other harmful microbes.

Cooking microgreens will definitely deplete them of precious enzymes and water-soluble vitamins. To make your microgreens as safe to eat raw as possible, it is important to maintain the hygiene of your growth containers and then rinse them properly before use. If you follow the guidelines for proper refrigeration, you will reduce the chances of bacteria and mold growing on your plants. Your plants will last up to a couple of weeks, preserving their taste and freshness (Mir et al., 2017).

Ideally, you'll eat microgreens raw. In this state, they contain the greatest amounts of nutrients, and they also have the most intense taste. However, you can also cook microgreens, as long as you don't boil them. If you don't want to add fresh microgreens into your meal, you can leave them to briefly steam.

Preferably, this will be a couple of minutes before you take the pot off the stove. This way, your greens will retain taste and freshness but also keep the valuable nutrients.

When adding microgreens to your meals, you can use stems and leaves, as long as you carefully rinse them of any remaining debris and germs. Whether or not you'll use the roots depends on the species. You can also blend your greens prior to adding them into dishes or crush them to release extra smell and flavor. Don't forget that you can mix as many varieties as you want!

With this in mind, we will now present you with a couple of ideas for cooking with microgreens. In the next section, you'll find instructions for incorporating microgreens into your daily meals.

TIPS AND IDEAS FOR
DELICIOUS MEALS

Y ou can enrich any meal with microgreens, adding flavors of your choosing and extra sass to the most common meals. In this section, we'll give you simple and easy ideas to incorporate microgreens into your daily diet. Following are the simplest ways to turn any meal into a body-regenerating treat:

Microgreen Pizza. By definition, pizza is a simple dish, and we're not against it when it comes to good nutrition. However, stacking a regular pizza with cheese, sausage, and pepperoni doesn't result in the most stomach-friendly meal. Instead, replacing the fatty ingredients with microgreen arugula, basil, onion, or spinach will result in a tasty treat and healthy meal.

However, it's important not to bake microgreens along with the pizza, or else you'll lose the majority of nutrients. Instead, add the amount you'd like a couple of minutes before taking the pizza out of the oven, which will give them a tasty crunchiness without killing the nutrients. Of course, you can always season a finished pizza with fresh microgreens, if that's what you prefer!

Burgers with microgreens. Burgers, sadly, have a notorious reputation for being unhealthy. However, if you prepare them with microgreens like arugula, kohlrabi, and cabbage, they'll have a rich flavor which will easily compensate for the lack of calories derived from carbs like buns or cheese.

Nourishing pesto. Aside from basil and onions, you can add pea shoots and sunflower to create a truly authentic, yet healthy and nutritious pesto. You can use this sauce either as an addition to pasta or as a salad dressing. You can also use this pesto to further season sandwiches and wraps.

Microgreen salsa. Salsa is yet another dish that's made for creativity and variety. Whichever microgreen you choose, from lemongrass, lemon, cinnamon basil, sunflower, or even spicier ones like peppercress, you can simply add them to the dish and create your own authentic recipe. This way, you'll come up with a perfect recipe that will go great with quesadillas, chips, tortilla, tacos, and many more.

Microgreen guacamole. Adding microgreen sunflower to your regular guacamole will make a super healthy dip for your chips and tacos. By all means, feel free to add any other plant you choose!

You can also add this guacamole to salads, sandwiches, wraps, and any other meal of your choosing.

Microgreen pancakes. If you enjoy your daily dose of pancakes, you'll find pea shoot microgreens to be a great addition to your daily treat. Simply blend the plant, adding chives and other savory greens into the batter. This will result in a delicious pancake! In addition, if you're cooking for children who tend to dislike veggies, as many do, this is a good way to disguise them into a delicious meal.

Microgreen pasta sauces. It's very simple to turn your average pasta sauce into a treat for your blood vessels and immune system, much like for the palate. Lemongrass, arugula, basil, garlic, zucchini, and others add delicious flavors to numerous sauces, from Bolognese, to pesto and carbonara. There's no exact measure when it comes to adding microgreens to pasta sauces. You can choose the amount based on your taste and preference and decide between blending, crushing, or adding them whole into the sauces. In addition, popping the plants into sauces, while they're still cooking, for no longer than a minute, will enhance the flavors without compromising the nutrients.

Microgreen omelet. A morning omelet with a touch of microgreen is a great way to boost your breakfast with precious proteins, vitamins, and iron. If you further add delicious greens, such as microgreen spinach, onions, and basil to a simple omelet, you'll benefit from an abundant boost of nutrients before your morning jog or a workout. This will set you up for a productive day, improving your energy levels and focus at work. Furthermore, the flavor of this meal will add a touch of the exotic and Mediterranean into an otherwise plain breakfast. You can add microgreens to your omelet by blending them and mixing into the eggs prior to frying, or you can crush them and sprinkle over the dish.

Microgreen soup. Soups are a great way to hydrate before a satisfying meal. Furthermore, they are a great way to fight off viruses when you are sick and to boost your immune system. To add microgreens to your soap, add them when the meal is already cooked to preserve the most nutrients. Leave the soup to cool down slowly while the precious plants steam inside of the pot, releasing flavors and nutrients. Sunflower, beans, onions, lemongrass, basil, radish, carrots, and any other microgreens you enjoy can be a great addition to your regular soup.

In this chapter, you learned more about adding microgreens to your daily diet. With this knowledge, you can now proceed to enjoy your delicious crops, with full certainty that you'll know how to use them properly and maintain their beneficial properties. This will make your efforts worthwhile, as you'll soon be able to see the health benefits with daily use.

First, you learned how to store microgreens in your kitchen to best preserve their freshness, taste, and nutritional value. You learned that the best way to refrigerate your microgreens is to keep them in plastic bags, while protecting them from excess moisture and extreme temperatures. You learned that it's ideal to keep microgreens as far from the cooling vent as possible, and to keep the temperature of your refrigerator at the optimum 40 Fahrenheit.

In this chapter, you also learned how to properly cook microgreens. While there are some crops that handle high temperatures well, most of them aren't suitable to cook and bake. Instead, it's enough to add them to a meal that's already finished cooking, allowing them to steam and release their flavors as the meal cools down. In addition, you learned that you can also blend the greens into your juices and sauces to intensify the flavor of ordinary meals.

After that, you learned about the abundance of ways to incorporate microgreens into your daily diet. First, you learned that, in order to benefit from microgreens, you should consume them at least once a day, preferably multiple times per day. You also learned that the highest concentration and flavor is in the fresh herb, meaning that you'll get the highest quality use if you pluck the small amounts you need and use them right away.

You also can use them to make salads, sandwiches, wraps, and juices, and also add them to pastas, sauces, soups, and all other meals. With an abundance of microgreens to choose from, it is only up to you to decide which you'll enjoy the most.

Whichever your choice is, there's no doubt that you can use the abundance of flavors to enhance the taste and nutritional value of your meals. After that, we gave you some creative ideas about how you can incorporate microgreens into your usual daily meals. We focused on the simplest meals that most people have daily, aiming to provide you with simple guidelines regarding adding microgreens to common meals like omelets, soups, pizza, pasta, and others. With this in mind, it will be effortless for you to use microgreens, as you won't have to jump through hoops to discover new, complex recipes. We aimed for simplicity, which we believe is the best strategy to create a diet that is healthy, satisfying, and easy to maintain.

Now that you have everything you need to grow and use microgreens, perhaps you are interested in turning them into a business. The following chapter will further explain how you can start a business with microgreens, giving you simple and useful instructions on how to start your brand and which supplies to obtain.

CHAPTER 6:
MARKETING
MICROGREENS

I f you're wondering whether or not you can profit from growing microgreens, the simple and sweet answer is YES. You can turn growing microgreens into a business if you are thoughtful, organized, and well informed.

Starting a business can seem intimidating, but with the right guidance, you will find it not only manageable but also empowering. This is a great time to start marketing microgreens, as their popularity is at its peak.

They are considered to be a completely new category of foods, with plenty of science to back them up. With enormous nutritional value, they can become a source of a profitable business.

In this chapter, you will find out more about marketing microgreens. The last chapter of this book will show you how to start a business with microgreens, giving you all the information you need for a good start and a profitable outcome.

When thinking about their profitability and costs, many farmers are already creating their six-figure microgreen businesses, and so can you. Microgreen cultivation can be highly profitable, and it isn't at all difficult. Once you learn how to cultivate your first crops, you will easily move on to creating bulk amounts.

However, the tricky question remains about how to sell them, how to create your selling price, and what exactly to do in order to profit from them. The calculations behind any microgreen business are important to weigh your profits against costs and keep your business growing long term.

First, we will answer the question of if and which microgreens are marketable. As you already learned, microgreens are popular, albeit very gentle and sensitive to environmental conditions. Everything, from production to packaging, needs to be carefully planned to yield the best quality product.

Profitability is an important part of every business, including this one. For this reason, we will give you insight into the production economics of microgreens. We will give you some advice on what you can do to save while growing bulk amounts.

There are multiple reasons why microgreens can

become an easy source of consistent income, mainly due to swift growth and easy harvesting, which can secure a steady supply of marketable produce all year long. Unlike other crops, microgreens aren't bound to seasonal conditions, as they can be grown in controlled environments. In this chapter, we'll explain the exact benefits of starting a business with microgreens and give you smart tips to leverage these advantages.

Next, you will find the exact calculations of profit and start-up costs. Moreover, we will review the exact list of tools and supplies that you need for bulk cultivation. With this in mind, you will easily prepare everything you need to start growing large quantities of microgreens that you will later market.

A great benefit from starting a microgreen business comes from the low cost of tools and supplies, and we'll give you exact tips to obtain everything you need quickly and easily.

Aside from that, we will give you more information on selling microgreens. Selling microgreens isn't difficult as the demand for them is high. However, there's still some specific things you need to know about profiling your customers and advertising your business.

First, we will tell you how to evaluate your competition to find out more about your own business goals, after which you will start tracing potential clients to present your business to. Moreover, we will show you how to use customer and client feedback to improve your own practices.

Last, but not least, we will give you a detailed presentation about common legal requirements revolving around cultivating microgreens. Here, you will find out what the standards and certifications are that you need to follow for producing and selling microgreens legally and safely. This will help you consider the costs and efforts that will go into navigating the legal and administrative side of your business.

As you reach the end of this book, it's time that you find out how to make your efforts profitable and turn your kitchen hobby into a nine-to-five job. In the following section, we will give you the exact explanation for how and why you can profit from microgreens.

CAN MICROGREENS BE PROFITABLE?

When thinking about the profitability of microgreens, keep in mind that you do your math properly. So far, you've learned about the benefits of microgreens and the ways to grow them. But, from a business point of view, money is an important factor.

THE PRODUCTION ECONOMICS

When it comes to the economics of production, it's important to know that the majority of growers use inexpensive tools, such as trays, as well as benches and tables. You don't have to invest heavily into your supplies because the main things that affect the quality of produce include environmental influences.

The majority of successful cultivators use LED fluorescent lights. These lights are indoor-growing friendly. Also, experienced cultivators water the plants using filtered water, which removes harmful chemicals and chloride.

Additionally, a part of good practice is to add seaweed extract to the water, which will provide additional nutrients for the seeds. You will need to provide dark environments for germination and then move the germinated crops to trays, moving them into locations that contain better lighting.

Most growers apply potting soil blends. They either use soil as a medium, or fabric mats like burlap, if they use hydroponic. Most successful growers say that retail buyers such as upscale grocery stores and restaurants chefs are their best customers.

HOW MUCH CAN
YOU PROFIT?

I f you're a farmer, keep in mind that micro-greens are among the most profitable crops for you to grow. They don't need a lot of space and usually average $50 in selling price per pound. This price can even increase depending on the de-mand and competition. Microgreens are also great for smaller growers and small farms. You can grow them in storage boxes or shipping containers and place them in common areas like basements and garages to earn potentially six figures.

START-UP COSTS
AND SUPPLIES

Microgreens are a good business opportunity because the initial investment is very low, as you can use supplies you already have at home and obtain seeds very cheaply. In addition, the produce is ready for harvesting very quickly, meaning that you can see the first coin from your labor in only a couple of weeks.

When it comes to start-up costs, account for spending an average $2 per tray, including seed and soil. For starters, you can offer your services to only a single restaurant until you're skillful enough for larger scale produce. You can then expand to offering your produce in farmers' markets and increase production according to your own abilities. Another advantage of marketing microgreens is a fast turnaround time.

As already mentioned, microgreens take only up to a couple of weeks to harvest, which allows you to maximize operational efficiency and experiment with different techniques and varieties. This allows you to quickly upscale your production or reduce it if your sales start to drop.

Another advantage of commercial microgreen growing is that they are a year-round supply. They can be a source of consistent income, particularly if you are already familiar with agriculture and farming. If you are a farmer, microgreens can be a great way to keep your business running during the winter and supply additional income.

Microgreens are also high-value crops due to their enormous nutritional value. The plants are abundant with nutrients and vitamins, which makes them appealing to upscale restaurants as they make high end ingredients that serve as an incentive to selling expensive meals. This means that they are a very profitable product.

When it comes to the space you need to obtain, keep in mind that this business is very space economical. On average, growers produce around 50 pounds of microgreens per 60-square-foot space every two weeks with an average price between $20 and $50 per pound. This provides a profit of around $2,000 monthly. According to this math, you can profit around $100 to $160 per square meter, or $30 to $50 per square foot. Account for investing in your equipment, as well as optimizing your processes when calculating your price. On average, each individual tray that measures 10x20 inches in size will produce up to six ounces, which equals between 140 to 170 grams on aver-age

You can take up microgreen production by in-vesting anywhere from 15 minutes to a couple of hours every day. You will also need to account for the time that it takes to harvest and sell the prod-ucts.

However, a six-figure business will require full-time work. You will also have to start thinking about employing people to help you with pro-duction. Microgreens are a great business oppor-tunity because they are highly adjustable, and you can determine the amount that you want to produce depending on the income you want to achieve and the time you can set aside for growing them.

Here's a list of essential supplies that you will need to start your business:

- You will need a light fixture that uses two bulbs or four feet of fluorescent light. You will also need a couple of fluorescent bulbs.

- At a minimum, you will need 16 trays that average 10x20 inches in size. You will grow eight plates of microgreens on a four-foot setup per week, and you can increase this amount depending on the time and resources you have.

- Paper towels are another supply you will need. However, they are so cost friendly that you can obtain large quantities for only a couple of dollars.

- You will also need a spray bottle, which is essentially something that you don't have to invest in as you probably already have it in your home.

- You will need seeds, preferably starting with radish, as they are easy and fastest to grow. Invest some extra money into organic seeds because they are perceived to be of the highest value and will result in the highest-quality produce.

- You will also need a scale to measure produce well before packaging. You can use a regular kitchen scale to do this.

- Sharp scissors and knives for harvesting are also necessary.

- Regular potting soil will be enough for beginners.

- You will also need a timer that you will use to turn your lights on and off as needed.

- You will need a small fan to ventilate your crops, which will prevent contamination and molding.

- You can also get a regular, cheap watering can.

You can think about whether or not you want to get the new supplies or use the ones you already have.

HOW TO SELL MICROGREENS

T he first thing I want to tell you is to account for every penny when turning your microgreens hobby into a business. You first need to realize that your selling price will be at least a 100% markup from your initial investment.

Your price will have to cover taxes, shipping, production costs, and everything else that goes into growing and selling the product from point A, which is supplying seeds, to point B, which is getting the product to your customer and charging them for it. Everything needs to be accounted for in the price.

Adding to that, a portion must be included to compensate for your time and effort. After all, this is your profit for doing this business. Another thing to consider is that microgreens don't last long when refrigerated. Unless consumed fresh, they will lose plenty of nutrients and replenishing substances that will deplete them of their value. One way to overcome this obstacle is to sell your produce at local markets.

This way, you will offer freshly grown plants that will contain the highest value. Many small farmers have grown their business to steady full-time jobs.

However, before you start, you have to be completely educated and aware of everything that goes into the successful production of microgreens. Your product needs to be of the highest quality to be marketable. You have competition, and that competition has many advantages over you when it comes to business knowledge and creating quality microgreen produce. Now, again to the business side of things.

EVALUATE
COMPETITION

First things first, you will have to identify your competitors and customers. The former are the ones you want to exceed in quality of offering, and the latter are the ones you want to target when selling. To evaluate your competition, it is wise to first order a couple of batches from them and evaluate their businesses. Look into their prices, quantities, and quality of product. Other than that, look into their processes of growing, cultivating, harvesting, storing, and everything else to discover the things you want to emulate and the things that should be done better.

REACH OUT TO POTENTIAL CLIENTS

Once you start your business, you can then reach out to local restaurants and offer samples as your first sale. It is your choice whether you want to offer small samples for free or introduce yourself as an existing business and suggest a business deal. You will have to target the restaurant chef, who is the main person to decide whether or not a particular supplier or a product is worth the investment. You shouldn't waste your time reaching out to managers and other staff. You can contact as many restaurants as you can manage, but preferably, you will target those that are most popular and most successful. Always keep in mind when planning your produce to preserve extra supplies for free distribution as samples.

Additionally, be willing to openly speak about your prices and storing conditions because this will present you as a reliable and honest business.

ADVERTISE YOUR BUSINESS

Present your products well by creating pamphlets or sheets that include quality pictures and descriptions of your products. Another important business tip is to underpromise when it comes to the quality of your product and then deliver more than expected. Long term, this can help you develop stable relationships with your clients.

Also, keep in mind that, if you are offering to restaurants, their chefs are quite busy and won't have a lot of time for you. Instead, you will only have a couple of minutes of their time to taste your product and to share the most vital information, such as how much you can supply daily, and at what price, the shipping details, whether your produce is organic and fresh, and how soon you can deliver the desired quantities. Be prepared to give this two-to-three-minute presentation. Take some time to practice it.

BE FLEXIBLE

In addition, if you are competing with other suppliers for the same client, try to find out if they have any complaints and what they appreciate the most about their current supplier. If your potential client has complaints about their current supplier, look for those as a source of obstacles you want to surpass with your own offering, and use the information about features that they appreciate to emulate in your own production and surpass the competition. Take regular pictures of your farm and produce to make yourself as accessible and personable as possible. You want to advertise these photos in your online store, attracting companies, grocery stores, distributors and farmers' markets. For people to buy from you they need to be well aware of your presence.

GET TO KNOW
YOUR CUSTOMERS

For your business to be successful, you really need to know your customers well. First things first, you need to be informed about their expectations and opinions on microgreens.

You need to focus on what they perceive to be beneficial, and what they perceive to be challenging about their use, and then use this information to adjust your own produce. Once your business starts to grow, and you start to gain more customers, you want to frequently get updates from them to find out if they have any opinions to share or suggestions for improvement.

Observe customer responses religiously, and think about applying any criticism to improve your business. One of the biggest mistakes that business owners make is being defensive about criticism. Receiving criticism with a defensive attitude will show your customers that you don't care about them but instead want to preserve your own face, which is not a good look. While you should aim to preserve your reputation and standing, you should always apply customers' feedback into your own processes. Make sure to note any special requests from your clients and customers regarding quality and varieties you are offering.

Are there any varieties that they desire that currently aren't a part of your production? Are there certain species you sell that aren't particularly popular? You want to consider these aspects so that you can offer it as the right product that your client needs.

Last, but not least, consider all other factors that affect profitability. Do your due diligence and research and discover what are the most profitable varieties to grow and sell. In addition, always be thoughtful of looking for better and more profit-friendly ways to grow and produce.

LEGAL AND OTHER CONSIDERATIONS

Before starting your business, it is important to be aware of essential legal considerations. If you want to be a successful business owner, there are plenty of standards and legalities you will have to abide by to run your business according to the law.

First things first, it is important that, from a legal point of view, there are certain health risks associated with plant production (Riggio et al., 2019) Food safety will remain one of your biggest concerns when producing microgreens. It is important to be aware of all the processes and applications that are necessary to provide safe ingredients.

When starting the microgreens business, you first need to learn more about food safety regulations. You will find plenty of documents online that provide information about different laws and duties you'll have to follow with production.

Depending on the government levels, whether the regulations are federal, provincial, or municipal, you will follow different requirements. To safely produce microgreen products for your consumers, when it comes to municipal standards, you will have to look into the individual laws and permits required in your own municipality. Usually, this includes development permits, local business licenses, and regulations.

You will also have to follow facility guidelines and requirements. Regulations often cover facility inspections and food handling permits, as well as safety training and courses for safe food production aimed at farmers. On the other hand, federal regulations often refer to safety and packaging requirements.

Whichever program you choose, you will have to abide by the OFFS program, as it is an essential part of providing your customers with healthy, safe, and sanitary products. Most customers and distributors require OFFS certification, which signifies that you follow legal requirements for safe and conscientious produce. You will also have to learn about food safety programs and requirements regarding plants, farming, preharvest handling, distribution, services, and provision of storage.

When it comes to microgreen risk assessment, it is intended to analyze potential safety risks and communicate them to growers so that they can follow the rules of best practice. These requirements cover potential hazards in terms of biological pathogens, pests and allergens, chemical hazards like cleaners, fertilizers, and pesticides, and physical hazards like water, glass, metal, nails, and debris.

When it comes to biological hazards, you will pay attention to risks associated with listeria, which is affected by ventilation and airflow. It also is impacted by the temperature of the facility. It is also relevant to whether the seeds you obtain possibly contain microorganisms. For this, it is important to source your seeds from a reputable supplier.

When it comes to pests, like rodents, insects, etc., it is relevant which measures you will apply to prevent them from contaminating your produce. This includes measures such as cleaning, proper storage, and other protocols to prevent and treat possible past infections.

When it comes to chemical hazards, you will need to pay attention to whether you're storing any chemicals in the same area where you grow your microgreens. While this is not desirable, you should aim to clear your facility of any chemicals and instruct your staff to follow the best hygiene practices.

When it comes to physical hazards, you should pay attention to whether your growing racks can support the weight of the plants. You will also have to pay attention to the quality of lighting and whether it has been made with shatterproof materials. You will also have a mitigation proto-col, in case your light bulbs shatter in the growing area.

Also, this includes the protocols you will estab-lish for disposal of microgreens that may have been contaminated, and to clear your production facility of any construction materials. Aside from that, further legal and taxation requirements de-pend mainly on the individual town, state, or re-gion, which is something you can learn about by talking to local authorities.

In this chapter, you learned valuable information regarding marketing microgreens and creating your own brand and business. First you learned that you need to approach the venture with common business smarts by paying attention to profitability. While passion and vision are both important for growing a successful microgreen business, it is also necessary to pay attention to your profits, as they are what keep your business and income going.

First, you found out that microgreens are highly profitable because they only require the use of tools that you most likely already have. It's likely that you will only have to invest in a small num-ber of trays and optimal lighting for your plants. Aside from that, you can significantly reduce your costs by planning the space in which you'll cultivate the plants for their best growth

You also learned that you will have to account for everything that goes into production and delivery of microgreens so that your business is sustainable. While microgreens have low start-up costs, these costs will increase as your business grows.

To keep your business up and running, you found out that you will have to find good ways to present yourself. You learned that you will have to reach out to restaurant owners, chefs, and showcase your products in farmers' markets to advertise your business. You also learned the ways to make yourself noticeable, like printing out images and pamphlets, giving out free samples, and many more. Perhaps, the most important factor that will determine the success of your business is your relationship with customers. You will grow as a brand if you learn how to follow your customers' opinions and feedback regarding the quality and taste of your product.

You also learned that researching the competition and your potential customers will give you the information about how you should adjust your processes and the choice of varieties to best cater to the market.

Last but not least, you learned about the important health and safety standards that apply across most states. When it comes to growing microgreens, you learned that you'll have to pay attention to different hazards, from physical and chemical, to hygiene factors that might contaminate your produce.

Now, as you're finishing this book, I want to leave you with some simple advice to start small and slowly build up your own production. Before you get to know and practice cultivation of microgreens, you shouldn't order bulk quantities of seeds. Instead, do your research first, and discover what the most popular varieties are and start growing small amounts until you get used to them, and master small-scale cultivation.

After that, you can move on to bulk cultivation and order a greater amount of seeds. This will ensure that you grow the plants with the highest level of success and quality, as quality comes first. It's essential that you remain devoted to giving your plants proper environmental conditions to thrive.

As you finish this book, we hope to have given you exactly the right information you need to start growing, using, and marketing microgreens right now!

CONCLUSION

Congratulations! You finished your manual on how to grow and market microgreens successfully. This book aimed to present you with the benefits of cultivating and using microgreens. Hopefully, we've given you all the information you need to understand the value of these gentle, yet powerful, plants, and how to include them in your everyday diet.

The main purpose of this book was to show you not only the benefits of microgreens but also the simplicity and beauty of growing them on your own. Hopefully, while reading this book, you learned that microgreens are extremely easy to grow, if you follow the right steps and guidelines.

As you reach the end of this book, you now know everything you need about these small, yet valuable plants, to not only grow them for boosting your own health but to start your own business. This book is aimed to give you easy and comprehensive instructions on growing and marketing microgreens.

We started off by first explaining what microgreens are. In this book, you learned that microgreens are young versions of regular vegetables and herbs that are germinated and harvested at the young stage of their growth. You also learned that they have grown in popularity during the past couple of decades, mainly due to health benefits and their delicious taste. In fact, they're considered to be a luxurious condiment by high-end restaurants, and have been featured on television, in cookbooks, and even used to treat illnesses!

In the second chapter of this book, you found out the truth behind that popularity. You learned that science shows that microgreens not only contain enormous amounts of nutrients compared to adult plants, but also have the potential to support healing from many illnesses, like kidney disease, weakness of the immune system, cardiovascular disease, obesity, diabetes, and others. You learned that these small plants may be tender in appearance, but that they are, in fact, up to a hundred times more potent than some of the healthiest vegetables!

In fact, as you found out, they contain enormous amounts of antioxidants, which are known to improve body functioning and regeneration of your cells. This important finding showed you that you can use microgreens to boost your body's natural ability to heal and rejuvenate. As you learned, antioxidants can help your body get rid of free radicals, the compounds that impair your health on a cellular level. Using microgreens, you can boost the health of your cells to help them get rid of faults and start growing fresh, healthy tissues.

You learned that microgreens pile up nutrients as they get ready to mature and grow into an adult plant. If you're careful enough to pluck them at the right time, you'll get a vitamin-packed batch of freshly harvested plants that you can eat raw, put in meals, or mix into smoothies.

You also learned that the nutritional value of microgreens greatly depends on their environment. You learned that lighting, temperature, handling, and fertilization have a lot to do with the quality of the end product. In this book, we presented you with research findings that showed that insufficient light, water, too high or low temperatures, and improper soil can completely deplete the valuable nutrients inside microgreens.

For these reasons, we briefly described the optimal conditions needed for the healthy growth of microgreens. You learned that they thrive best at room temperature and in moderate light. You also learned that they need to be consistently misted with filtered water, but not too much, or else they'll start growing mold and bacteria.

You also learned that the choice of seeds can affect the quality of an adult plant. In the second chapter of this book, we explained all possible health benefits from using microgreens. Once we convinced you of the enormous possible benefits of microgreens, we went on to help you choose the best seeds and crops.

We showed you how to decide on the crops you want to cultivate, by laying out the list of those that are most popular and most suitable for beginners. You learned that growing these plants costs next to nothing and that there are microgreens that are so simple to grow that they don't demand anything else other than soaking and placing on a paper towel! We also presented you with numerous types and individual species, describing their looks, taste, nutritional value, and methods for growing.

Knowing this will help you decide which ones you like best and which are the ones you'll choose to start cultivating. For beginners, we recommended growing a limited amount of varieties, preferably those you already enjoy as grown vegetables. This way, you'll be sure to like and enjoy your lush produce. In addition, we recommended growing only the amount you'll use up right away, as storing and preserving microgreens will take some exercise.

In this book, you also learned that purchasing the best seeds is extremely important to ensuring the quality of your plants. You learned that seed quality is important not only because of the genetic foundation for healthy plants but also for your microgreens to be free of toxic chemicals and be organic. For this, you learned that it's important to purchase only from reputable sellers. In addition, you learned how to distinguish non-GMO from organic and untreated seeds. We recommended purchasing only organic, untreated, and non-GMO seeds, since they have the greatest potential for high germination rates.

As you learned, germination rates determine how many of your seeds will sprout and proceed to grow. For highest germination, we recommended only top-quality suppliers, which you'll discover by researching brands and reading the information from their websites.

Once you fully understood microgreens and their benefits, we went on to explain and instruct you on how to properly grow them. In the fourth chapter of this book, you learned exactly how to grow microgreens. You learned that, in order to get all of the tools and supplies needed for this hobby, you will need plenty of containers, water, water filters, growth media, fertilizers, and sources of light to keep your seed growing and your plants well nourished.

However, the process of planting remains simple, consisting only out of presoaking the seeds, filling a container with a growth medium, and transferring the seeds. However, different specics, as you learned, differ when it comes to presoaking necessity, days needed to sprout, and harvest times. By looking into the information given in this manual, you'll be able to pick the plants that will be ready for harvesting roughly at the same time, making it easier for you to enjoy them all at once!

Next, we explained the exact process of growing microgreens. You learned how to plant the microgreens step by step, as well as to how to harvest them and care for them after harvesting to preserve their quality.

After that, we showed you the best strategies for consuming microgreens. You learned about the abundance of simple ways to grow and include microgreens in your daily diet, such as to use them to make juices and smoothies, different meals, sandwiches, salads, and wraps, and also pasta sauces and soups.

We gave you a couple of simple and sustainable tips and ideas for everyday meals that you will be able to use effortlessly. With these instructions, you'll add a variety of interesting tastes into your kitchen, while supporting your body as it regenerates and rejuvenates.

After that, we gave you instructions on how to turn your hobby into a business. We presented you with the reasons why microgreens are profitable and what you can do to start your own business. First, you learned that one of the reasons why microgreens are so highly profitable lies in the fact that they grow quickly, easily, and through the entire year.

You can choose any species you want and grow them regardless of the season. As you are the one controlling the conditions, you have the power to grow as many or as few microgreens as you want.

However, in order to create a business, you'll need to calculate the possible profits depending on the amounts of produce you can cultivate and the quality you can offer. As you learned, it is of grave essence to first focus on growing healthy, delicious herbs.

After you've mastered the art of microgreen cultivation, you can then move on to offering your produce to different clients, like restaurants, or sell them fresh in farmers' markets. As you learned, microgreens can easily become a full-time job. That is, if you're willing to learn and treat your crops with adequate care.

As you reach the final words of this book, we want to thank you for your time.

Hopefully, we've answered all your questions, and given you all instructions you need for the successful growing of microgreens.

OTHER BOOKS BY GORDON L. ATWELL

AQUAPONICS FOR BEGINNERS

HYDROPONICS FOR BEGINNERS

REFERENCES

Brazaitytė, A., Viršilė, A., Samuolienė, G., Jank-auskienė, J., Sakalauskienė, S., Sirtautas, R., ... & Duchovskis, P. (2016, May). Light quality: Growth and nutritional value of microgreens under indoor and greenhouse conditions. *VIII International Symposium on Light in Horticulture*, Article 1134_37, 277-284.

Choe, U., Yu, L. L., & Wang, T. T. (2018). The science behind microgreens as an exciting new food for the 21st century. *Journal of Agricultural and Food Chemistry*, 66(44), 11519-11530.

Crispy Edge. (n.d.). *Why are microgreens such a popular ingredient?* https://crispyedge.com/2018/04/17/why-are-microgreens-such-a-popular-ingredient/

Di Gioia, F., Mininni, C., & Santamaria, P. (2015). How to grow microgreens. *Microgreens. Ecologica editore, Bari*, 51-79.

Fresh Origins. (n.d.). *Microgreens facts*. http://www.freshorigins.com/microgreens-facts/

Kyriacou, M. C., Rouphael, Y., Di Gioia, F., Kyratzis, A., Serio, F., Renna, M., ... & Santamaria, P. (2016). Micro-scale vegetable production and the rise of microgreens. *Trends in Food Science & Technology, 57*, 103-115.

Mir, S. A., Shah, M. A., & Mir, M. M. (2017). Microgreens: Production, shelf life, and bioactive components. *Critical reviews in food science and nutrition, 57*(12), 2730-2736.

Mumm's Sprouting Seeds. (n.d.). *Growing a microgreen business.* Sprouting. http:// sprouting.com/ growing_a_microgreen_business.html#a16558

Riggio, G. M., Wang, Q., Kniel, K. E., & Gibson, K. E. (2019). Microgreens—A review of food safety considerations along the farm to fork continuum. *International Journal of Food Microbiology, 290*, 76-85.

Samuolienė, G., Brazaitytė, A., Jankauskienė, J., Viršilė, A., Sirtautas, R., Novičkovas, A., ... & Duchovskis, P. (2013). LED irradiance level affects growth and nutritional quality of Brassica microgreens. *Open Life Sciences, 8*(12), 1241-1249.

Schiffler, A. (2019, March 6). The beginner's guide to start growing microgreens. Herbs at Home. https://herbsathome.co/the-beginners-guide-to-start-growing-microgreens/

Xiao, Z., Lester, G. E., Luo, Y., & Wang, Q. (2012). Assessment of vitamin and carotenoid concentrations of emerging food products: Edible microgreens. *Journal of Agricultural and Food Chemistry, 60*(31), 7644-7651.

Made in the USA
Monee, IL
27 July 2020